VAN BUREN DISTRICT LIBRARY
DECATUR, MICHIGAN 49045

THE SLOW WORK OF GOD

D1621877

DISCARDED

THE
SLOW WORK
OF GOD

LIVING THE GOSPEL TODAY

THOMAS P. RAUSCH, SJ

Paulist Press
New York / Mahwah, NJ

The poems, "Praying," on pages 21–22, and "The Vast Ocean Begins Just Outside Our Church: The Eucharist" on page 49 are from *Thirst* by Mary Oliver. Copyright © 2006 by Mary Oliver. Reprinted by permission of Beacon Press, Boston.

Chapter 15 "The Slow Work of God" was previously published as an article "Take and Read: Tattoos on the Heart" in the National Catholic Reporter online edition on April 4, 2016. (https://www.ncronline.org/blogs/ncr-today/take-and-read-tattoos-heart). Used with permission.

The Scripture quotations contained herein are from the New Revised Standard Version: Catholic Edition, Copyright © 1989 and 1993, by the Division of Christian Education of the National Council of the Churches of Christ in the United States of America. Used by permission. All rights reserved.

Cover image by Leelakajonkij/Shutterstock.com
Cover design by Phyllis Campos
Book design by Lynn Else

Copyright © 2017 by Thomas P. Rausch, SJ

All rights reserved. No part of this publication may be reproduced, stored in a retrieval system, or transmitted in any form or by any means, electronic, mechanical, photocopying, recording, scanning, or otherwise, without either the prior written permission of the Publisher, or authorization through payment of the appropriate per-copy fee to the Copyright Clearance Center, Inc., www.copyright.com. Requests to the Publisher for permission should be addressed to the Permissions Department, Paulist Press, permissions@paulistpress.com.

Library of Congress Cataloging-in-Publication Data
Names: Rausch, Thomas P., author.
Title: The slow work of God : living the gospel today / Thomas P. Rausch, SJ.
Description: New York : Paulist Press, 2017. | Includes bibliographical references.
Identifiers: LCCN 2016054326 (print) | LCCN 2017015711 (ebook) | ISBN 9781587687167 (Ebook) | ISBN 9780809153503 (pbk. : alk. paper)
Subjects: LCSH: Christian life—Catholic authors. | Spiritual life—Catholic Church. | Ignatius, of Loyola, Saint, 1491-1556. Exercitia spiritualia. | Francis, Pope, 1936–
Classification: LCC BX2350.3 (ebook) | LCC BX2350.3 .R38 2017 (print) | DDC 248.4/82—dc23
LC record available at https://lccn.loc.gov/2016054326

ISBN 978-0-8091-5350-3 (paperback)
ISBN 978-1-58768-716-7 (e-book)

Published by Paulist Press
997 Macarthur Boulevard
Mahwah, New Jersey 07430

www.paulistpress.com

Printed and bound in the
United States of America

For Cecilia

CONTENTS

Contents

ACKNOWLEDGMENTS

The title for this book, *The Slow Work of God,* comes from a prayer by the French Jesuit Pierre Teilhard de Chardin; I first came across it in Greg Boyle's fine book *Tattoos on the Heart: The Power of Boundless Compassion.*

I owe thanks to a number of friends and colleagues who helped bring this work to completion. Michael Downey read the manuscript and offered helpful comments. Cecilia González-Andrieu sharpened my comments on art. Cecilia Chang encouraged me to move beyond a "churchy" book to do something more spiritual. Michael Daley and Dianne Bergant, CSA, graciously allowed me to include my article on Greg Boyle's book, published earlier in NCR Online and soon to appear in a book. I'm continually grateful to Paul McMahon for his friendship, encouragement, and always careful editing. And thanks to our graduate assistants, Christian Palmer-Newton and William Josh Perry, for their help in reviewing the page proofs. To all these friends and colleagues, I offer my appreciation and thanks.

INTRODUCTION

One of the privileges of our Jesuit life is that each year we are given eight days to spend in retreat. It is a privilege because not everyone is able to take a week out of their busy schedules or jobs to spend time in silence and prayer. The community is generous in giving us this opportunity. It is indeed a luxury, but it is also for most of us a vital intermission from the everyday and the routine, a time of grace, and sometimes of struggle.

A retreat means putting aside normal business and concerns and entering into silence. Leaving one's ordinary residence in parish or school gives one a chance to leave behind the world of asphalt, glass, and steel and get close again to nature, to walk under the great blue sky, smell the earth, and delight in the Creator's great palette of colors evident in field and flower. It is a time to sense the mystery of the divine, to seek God's face, to rekindle hope in God's promise to be always with us. It is a time to grow in one's discipleship.

A Jesuit's retreat is usually informed by the *Spiritual Exercises* of St. Ignatius. That doesn't mean following literally all the minute directions of his little book. For most of us, it means spending a week contemplating the life of Jesus in the context of the mystery of salvation. The retreat usually begins with the First Principle and Foundation, with its consideration of spiritual freedom or what Ignatius speaks of as indifference before all created things, and moving on to the First Week's consideration of the sin, in the hope of experiencing oneself again as a forgiven sinner, loved by a merciful God.

From there the retreatant usually moves to focus on the life, death, and resurrection of Jesus, as outlined in the subsequent three weeks. Many follow the method of Ignatian contemplation, a consideration of the "mysteries" in the life of Christ—the events, sayings, parables, and teachings, and the key meditation on the kingdom of Christ, with its call to discipleship—entering imaginatively into them. For some, it's enough simply to remain quietly and attentively in God's presence, to be with Jesus in the focus of the will and longings of the heart, to rest in his presence. To live in Christ also means to enter into his paschal mystery, living each day in obedience to the Father, sharing in his passage through death to life eternal. Thus the *Exercises* are radically christocentric.

Jesus poured out the Spirit on his own, the Holy Spirit that helps us perceive God's mysterious presence and activity—God's grace—in the world and in our lives. Spirituality describes our efforts to organize our lives in openness to the Spirit, making us sensitive to God's work that heals our wounds, changes our hearts, and promises us eternal life.

For those who have truly encountered Jesus and responded to his call to be in his company, to be "in Christ" is to be in his Body, the Church. For St. Paul, the two are inseparable. Life in the Church means a life nourished by the word of God, celebrated in Eucharist, and expressed in service of others. It means sharing in Christ's priesthood, offering our struggles, sacrifices, and crosses with him in one gift to the Father.

Finally, Jesus sends his disciples out to proclaim the good news to others, to witness to God's presence in our midst, bringing people together, overcoming divisions, loving in deeds and not just in words as Ignatius says at the end of the *Exercises* in his Contemplation for Obtaining Love. In the words of Pope Francis, all the members of the people of God in virtue of their baptism are called to be "missionary disciples," actively engaged in the task of evangelization (EG 119ff.).

Introduction

This is the goal of the *Spiritual Exercises*: to join with Christ in his salvific mission.

The present book is designed for spiritual reading or a retreat. It offers brief meditations and short reflections on the mysteries of the Christian life, inspired by the *Spiritual Exercises* and by three important texts of Pope Francis: his apostolic exhortation on the joy of the gospel, *Evangelii gaudium* (2013); his encyclical on the environment, *Laudato si'* (2015); and his apostolic exhortation on the family, *Amoris laetitia* (2016). The pope's own spirituality has been deeply shaped by his Jesuit formation. Though called to the Chair of Peter late in his life, he has labored to renew and reform the Church and to call all Christians to a deeper sense of the gospel's grace, which illumines and empowers the Christian life. He emphasizes particularly the mercy of God.

Part 1 begins with the mystery of God, the God who speaks in silence, is glimpsed in the beautiful, and awakens our hope that the deepest desires of our hearts will one day find fulfillment. Part 2 focuses on the person of Jesus, the Word of God become flesh, his teaching, and his paschal mystery into which we enter through baptism. Part 3 takes up the works of the Holy Spirit, personifying the presence and action of God in the Old Testament, animating the life of believers, and promising them salvation. Part 4 moves to the Church, Christ's Body, which makes his presence and action visible in history and draws us into the very life of God. Part 5 seeks to show how what Pope Francis calls the Joy of the Gospel can transform our own personal journeys and the world that the Church seeks to serve. Running through the book are examples of those "graced moments" when suddenly we become aware of God's grace, beauty, or presence breaking into our lives. They are transformative moments, always to be cherished.

Abbreviations

DOCUMENTS OF VATICAN II

DV   *Dei verbum*: Dogmatic Constitution on Divine Revelation
GS   *Gaudium et spes*: Pastoral Constitution on the Church in the Modern World
LG   *Lumen gentium*: Dogmatic Constitution on the Church
NA   *Nostra aetate*: Declaration on the Relationship of the Church to Non-Christian Religions
SC   *Sacrosanctum concilium*: Constitution on the Sacred Liturgy
UR   *Unitatis redintegratio*: Decree on Ecumenism

OTHER

EG   *Evangelii gaudium*: The Joy of the Gospel
WCC   World Council of Churches

PART I
GOD

1

THE HOLY

The story of Moses before the burning bush in the desert of Midian (Exod 3:1–12) is a classic. There is something both mysterious and frightening about his experience. He is drawn to this bush, on fire but not consumed. At the same time, Moses has encountered the holy. He hears a voice telling him, "Remove the sandals from your feet, for the place on which you are standing is holy ground." The proper response is reverence. One of the best descriptions of this experience comes from Rudolf Otto; he calls the holy or numinous the *mysterium fascinans et tremendum*.[1] It is a mystery that fascinates us; we find we are inescapably drawn to it. At the same time, its very otherness is awe-inspiring, even terrifying.

TRANSCENDENCE?

Our culture has lost its sense of the awe-inspiring character of the transcendent. We have little sense of the Divine Mystery. Gone are the symbols of God's presence in nature, religion, and our everyday lives. Our secular society has banished theology from the curricula of our universities and transcendent values from our civil discourse. But like the Freudian return of the repressed, a counterfeit transcendence surfaces in today's cinema. Rationality yields to a bogus supernaturalism. Movies are full of vampires, dragons, demonic figures, superheroes with special powers, and half-human spiritual masters like Yoda of the *Star Wars* movies. In the popular HBO television series *Game of Thrones*, religion has been reduced to ritual without content and conflated with magic. Where traces of the divine remain, it is no longer transcendent.

Our secular culture has domesticated the Divine Mystery, making it something safe and manageable. Rather than kneeling in reverence before the Other, we speak in familiar terms of my *personal* experience of God, or of a god that "is always there for me." But so often this is a god of our own making, a domesticated god who cannot challenge. This individualistic faith, with its cultural god, has been noted by religious sociologists. In their book *Habits of the Heart*, Robert Neelly Bellah and Richard Madsen call it "Sheilaism," after quoting a young nurse, to whom they gave the name Sheila Larson, "I believe in God. I'm not a religious fanatic. I can't remember the last time I went to church. My faith has carried me a long way. It's Sheilaism. Just my own little voice.... It's just try to love yourself and be gentle with yourself. You know, I guess, take care of each other. I think He would want us to take care of each other."[2] Wade Clark Roof observes that many find their experience of the sacred outside religious institutions; their approach to religion is highly subjective, exalting experience at the expense of religious authority.[3]

Christian Smith and Melinda Lundquist Denton identify what appears to be the most likely mainstream religion for our culturally post-Christian, individualistic, consumer society as "Moralistic Therapeutic Deism." Its god watches over life, wants people to be nice to each other and feel good about themselves, and does not need to be involved in their lives. This cultural god makes few demands, remains at a safe distance unless needed, and is essentially benign. Missing is the language of faithfulness, obligation, and obedience. There is no need for reverence, worship, or communal belonging. God is like us, only nicer and more powerful, and never to be feared.

THE BIBLICAL TRADITION

How different is the biblical tradition? The God of the Old Testament is transcendent, dwelling in a dense cloud on the holy mountain of Sinai, the God who says in Walter Kasper's translation, "I am the one who is there" (Exod 3:14).[4] God appears, challenges, and commands, but is not to be represented in any way. The God of Israel does not have a consort. The word *holy*, from the Hebrew root *kds*, means separate, set apart. It is used primarily of God, the "wholly other." God's holiness "is his radical difference and superiority to everything worldly and everything evil."[5] So different is God from human beings that to see God's face is to die (Judg 6:22–23; 13:22). When Moses asks the Lord to show him his glory, God answers, "You cannot see my face; for no one shall see me and live" (Exod 33:20). The Israelites were afraid to approach Moses after he had been in the presence of God because his face had become radiant, so he covered it with a veil (Exod 34:30–34).

This sense for God's otherness is also present in the New Testament. Peter, James, and John are terrified at the vision of the transfigured Jesus (Mark 9:6), and at the voice from the cloud identifying Jesus as "my beloved Son." They sense that God has drawn near and fall prostrate (Matt 17:5–6). In his Letter to the Romans, St. Paul breaks into a poetic celebration of the divine otherness:

> O the depth of the riches and wisdom and knowledge of God! How unsearchable are his judgments and how inscrutable his ways!
>
> "For who has known the mind of the Lord?
>   Or who has been his counselor?"
> "Or who has given a gift to him,
>   to receive a gift in return?"
>
> For from him and through him and to him are all things. To him be the glory forever. Amen. (Rom 11:33–36)

Persons, places, and things are called holy from their association with God. The Church is holy because of God's abiding presence in his people. God has given the Church holy gifts; the Word, the sacraments, especially the Eucharist. To this day, in the Orthodox tradition the deacon proclaims before communion, "God's holy gifts for God's holy people." Pope Francis's favorite image for the Church is "holy, faithful people of God" (*santo pueblo fiel de Dios*).

The Catholic tradition celebrates the presence of the holy with symbols, candles, art, and ritual. According to Tertullian, Christians have blessed themselves with the "sign of the cross" from the earliest days of the Church, on rising or retiring, going in or out of their houses, and when lighting the evening lamps.[6] We place icons or crucifixes in our homes. Our churches and chapels are holy places, with candles, statues, and holy water to remind us of the sacred. They are places for quiet prayer. Andrew Greeley sees Catholics as living "in an enchanted world, a world of statues and holy water, stained glass and votive candles, saints and religious medals, rosary beads, and holy pictures. But these Catholic symbols are mere hints of a deeper and more pervasive religious sensibility which inclines Catholics to see the Holy lurking in creation."[7]

Thomas Merton wrote, "Let there always be quiet, dark churches in which men can take refuge. Places where they can kneel in silence. Houses of God, filled with His silent presence."[8] Similarly, even before her conversion, when Dorothy Day was still living a Bohemian lifestyle in New York, she found herself frequently going to early morning Mass at St. Joseph's Church on Sixth Avenue; she "knelt in the back of the church, not knowing what was going on at the altar, but warmed and comforted by the lights and silence, the kneeling people and the atmosphere of worship. People have so great a need to reverence, to worship, to adore."[9]

Creation is holy because of the incarnation. In Jesus, the Divine Word became flesh. Christ is the Alpha and the Omega, the beginning and the goal of God's creative work. Catholicism has long resisted dualistic Manichean traditions that saw the material world as the work of a semi-eternal, evil deity. The fourth-century hymn ascribed to Nicetas of Remesiana, the *Te Deum*, celebrated Jesus who "did not disdain the virgin's womb," becoming one with us. Eastern Christianity has always seen humanity itself as transformed by the incarnation, while Western Christianity, shaped by Augustine's theology, places much more emphasis on the damage done it by original sin, demanding some kind of transaction done in Christ to restore humanity to God's grace. From this, it is not far to the Reformation doctrine of "total depravity," the idea that the entire human nature has been corrupted by sin so that humans are unable to choose to serve God. The Second Vatican Council taught that just as Jesus the Christ sanctified the Church through the Holy Spirit, so also each of the baptized, "whether belonging to the hierarchy, or being cared for by it, is called to holiness, according to the saying of the Apostle: 'For this is the will of God, your sanctification'" (LG 39).

A FRANCISCAN VISION

Pope Francis has a Franciscan vision of the holiness of creation. In his encyclical *Laudato si'*, he writes of God's declaring creation "very good," while every man and woman, created out of love and made in God's image and likeness, possesses an immense dignity (no. 65). He argues that human life is grounded in relationships close and intertwined with God, our neighbor, and the Earth. It is these relationships that the Genesis story of the fall sees as ruptured when the man and woman seek divine status for themselves. Francis appeals to his namesake, St. Francis of Assisi, whose love of nature was seen as healing that rupture. While careful not to divinize creation, he sees each creature as reflecting in its own way God's infinite wisdom and goodness, and therefore it is to be respected by humans, echoing the Psalms that invite all creatures to join in God's praise:

Praise him, sun and moon;
> praise him, all you shining stars!

Praise him, you highest heavens,
  and you waters above the heavens!

Let them praise the name of the LORD."

(Ps 148:3–5)

This beautiful world comes not from chaos or chance, but from God's loving plan, a God who is intimately present to each creature. Without diminishing the infinite distance between creatures and their Creator, each creature reflects God's presence, for the Spirit of God dwells within. And because all things are interconnected, care for nature is inseparable from fraternity, justice, and faithfulness to others. Thus, the pope argues that it is inconsistent "to combat trafficking in endangered species while remaining completely indifferent to human trafficking, unconcerned about the poor, or undertaking to destroy another human being deemed unwanted" (no. 91). Creation too is included in God's salvation in Christ, as we await and work for the day when "the Son himself will also be subjected to the one who put all things in subjection under him, so that God may be all in all" (1 Cor 15:28).

If God's holiness speaks of the divine transcendence, God's otherness, the incarnation means that God has drawn close to us, is present in our material world, and has entered into our lives in a personal way. Symbolizing the holy with ritual, sacred objects, and art makes us aware of that Divine Presence. We cherish these symbols, display them in our homes, rest in sacred spaces with reverence, mindful always of the God who created us and calls us into a future yet unknown.

2

Beauty

S ometimes when presiding at Mass in our campus chapel, I find myself struck by the beauty of our altar servers. These young people, undergraduate students, serve vested in white albs; they move with dignity through the service. Caught up in the solemnity of the liturgy, their self-consciousness fades away, revealing their youth, their perfect posture, and their beautiful faces. They are like angels in the sanctuary.

What is it about beauty that so holds us? A sunset that fills the evening sky with color, a snowcapped mountain, pine trees ascending to the tree line, the midnight heavens filled with stars, the happy faces of children running together in some secret game, the beauty of a human body. Beauty touches us deeply. Frederick Buechner relates a memory from when he was thirteen, sitting side by side with a girl of the same age on a seawall one evening at dusk in Bermuda:

> Our bare knees happened to touch for a moment, and in that moment I was filled with such a sweet panic and anguish of longing for I had no idea what that I knew my life could never be complete until I found it. ... It was the upward reaching and fathomlessly hungering, heart-breaking love for the beauty of the world at its most beautiful, and, beyond that,

for that beauty east of the sun and west of the moon which is past the reach of all but our most desperate desiring and is finally the beauty of Beauty itself, of Being itself and what lies at the heart of Being.[1]

THE WAY OF BEAUTY

When the Synodal Choir of the Moscow Patriarchate and the Sistine Chapel Choir gathered in the Basilica of Saint Mary Major for a joint concert, Pope Francis sent them a message of appreciation, quoting Dostoyevsky to the effect that "beauty will save the world." The Pope went on to explain that "music, painting, sculpture, architecture, in one word, beauty unites to make the celebrated faith grow, in prophetic hope, and in witnessed charity."[2] Similarly, in his apostolic exhortation *Evangelii gaudium*, Pope Francis speaks of the "way of beauty" (*via pulchritudinis*); he stressed the need for "a renewed esteem for beauty as a means of touching the human heart and enabling the truth and goodness of the Risen Christ to radiate within it. If, as Saint Augustine says, we love only that which is beautiful, the incarnate Son, as the revelation of infinite beauty, is supremely lovable and draws us to himself with bonds of love" (no. 167). Augustine realized that our desire for beauty is closely aligned to our desire, often unrecognized, for the transcendent.

ART AND THE BEAUTIFUL

Unlike the Jewish and Islamic traditions, which, taking literally the Decalogue prohibition of "graven" or sculpted images of the divine, forbids representing God or the human body, the Christian tradition has generally valued representational art. Think of Michelangelo's stunning work in the Sistine Chapel. But there are exceptions. The Eastern Church experienced outbreaks of iconoclasm in the eighth and ninth centuries, and some of the Reformers, particularly the followers of Calvin and Zwingli, were iconoclasts, destroying religious images, statues, and even stained glass windows. But art was part of the Christian tradition from the beginning. It begins to appear as early as the late second century, first in symbols found in the catacombs where Christians hid from persecution, later in more representational images. One of the most popular was an image of the Good Shepherd, portrayed as a beardless youth in a short tunic with a lamb draped over his shoulders. A third-century statue of this figure, from the Catacomb of Domitilla, is now in the Vatican Museum. It is a beautiful image of a God who comes searching for the lost, reaching out to creatures. Theologians like John of Damascus (c. 676–749) appealed to the incarnation to argue that the transcendent, invisible God becomes visible in the humanity of Jesus, and thus to an appreciation that our salvation is mediated by the material.

In his 1999 "Letter to Artists," Pope John Paul II uses a Polish lexical linkage to say that the work of a human craftsman (*twórca*) mirrors the image of God the Creator (*stwórca*). "With loving regard, the divine Artist passes on to the human artist a spark of his own surpassing wisdom, calling him to share in his creative power" (no. 1). The pope makes the point that just as God delights in his creation, finding it both good and beautiful,[3] so is beauty the visible form of the good. Indeed, beauty—genuine beauty—is the vocation of the artist. The pope sees an ethic, even spirituality, in the work of the artist, whose works of beauty enrich our cultural heritage and serve the common good.

The pope then takes his artist readers on a tour of art in the Christian tradition, starting with the appreciation of the beauty of the risen Christ, celebrated especially in the spirituality of the East, the signs of a new art in the Christic symbols found in the catacombs—the fish, the loaves, the shepherd, all part of a symbolic code used by the early Christians in times of persecutions. From there, he moves on to the basilicas that first adopted and then surpassed the architectural canons of the ancient world as the Church gained its freedom and began to build worship spaces, to the flowering of religiously inspired poetry and literature, Romanesque churches and abbeys and Gothic cathedrals reaching to the heavens in an architecture that united the functional with the creative, and finally, to Dante's *Divine Comedy*, all signs of an embodied faith. He argues that the Church needs art to open our vision to the world of the spirit, the transcendent; it needs architects to create beautiful spaces in which we can worship as well as music to touch our hearts and transform our liturgies. In this way, Christian art can help raise the hearts and minds of believers to contemplate God and the mysteries of salvation.

I remember seeing for the first time Salvador Dali's magnificent *Sacrament of the Last Supper* in the National Gallery in Washington, DC, when I was still very young, about nine years old. I was awestruck. From a technical standpoint, it is stunning; even more, it is rich in religious symbolism. The geometry of the windows forms a dodecahedron, a twelve-sided figure seen as a symbol of heaven.

There is a liturgical quality to the scene: On the table, a loaf of bread broken and a glass of wine; around the table, thirteen figures, the disciples, wrapped like monks in white habits, bowing in reverence. Jesus is in the center but not quite at the table; his figure is translucent, portrayed as a young man, beardless, as in some very early representations of the Good Shepherd. The focus is not historical, back to the Last Supper, but contemporary, the Eucharist, embraced by the Trinity. Jesus points upward to the Father, whose face is not to be seen (Exod 33:20), arms reaching out to embrace all, heaven and earth. A dove, symbol of the Spirit, sits over Jesus's left shoulder. The twelve-sided window opens the Supper to the world, symbolized by the Sea of Galilee (commentators say it's actually somewhere in Catalonia) in the background. Dali described it as the "first holy communion on earth."

In capturing or producing beauty, art can unveil, point beyond the familiar, and hold our attention. Imagine Michelangelo's magnificent *Pietà* in the Basilica of St. Peter's in Rome. Even when not beautiful in execution, art can put us in touch with the transcendent, for beauty and truth are interchangeable, both reflections of the absolute. Consider *Guernica*, Picasso's famous representation of the terror in a

Basque country village after a Nazi bombing during the Spanish civil war, or Francesco de Goya's works depicting the horrors of war during the invasion of Spain by Napoleon's troops in the Peninsular War of 1808–14. His *The Third of May 1808* portrays the execution by French soldiers of civilians defending Madrid. The horror in these two works is heartbreaking.

But creative works can also lie, offering glamor or skillful execution in place of beauty, facile answers, and scenes devoid of metaphor and real questions. As Cecilia González-Andrieu argues, we must be able to distinguish between what is truly beautiful and what is merely the seductively superficial "if beauty is to help lead us toward the good."[4] Too much of today's modern art is meant to shock, even to offend, in support of some private vision or ideology. One is reminded of Chris Ofili's *The Holy Virgin Mary*, an African Madonna surrounded by dabs of elephant dung and close-ups of female genitalia cut from pornographic magazines, or Nicki Johnson's portrait of Pope Benedict XVI made up of seventeen thousand colored condoms, exhibited at the Milwaukee Art Museum.

There is so much ugliness in the world. The horrors of war or terrorism leaving shattered structures, bleeding bodies, and broken hearts. Nature itself shows the signs of our self-preoccupation: rivers are polluted, sometimes poisoned, one once famously caught on fire; the blue of the skies turned to an impenetrable gray fog; trash and garbage strewn across fields and streams. Worse, we sometimes see late night TV reports on the poverty and degradation in which so many live today: sewage flowing down their streets, trash everywhere; jumbled dwellings of plywood and tin, nowhere a flower or tree. Pope Francis addresses the violence done to our earthly home in his encyclical letter *Laudato si'*.

ART AND THE SACRED

In his study of theological aesthetics, Richard Viladesau acknowledges that "art," what the "art world" calls art, is not always concerned with the creation of beauty. It may be concerned with mere self-expression, or with evoking or intensifying emotion, or with ornamentation, or simply with communicating something. But art can mediate the sacred when it embodies beauty, or even when it communicates profoundly human experiences such as fear, remorse, obligation, or desire, either through skillfully communicating the meaning of revelation or through evoking the holy. For beauty, he says, is an attribute to God.

> Beautiful art implicitly "speaks" of the divine exemplar, and at least raises the question of a transcendent human goal, eternal happiness in some kind of union with eternal Beauty. If that goal actually communicates itself as the gratuitously given sustaining dynamism of human existence, it is experienced precisely as loveable, desirable, beautiful. Hence beauty is a necessary attribute of grace and revelation, as it is of God's self that is communicated in these realities; and the beauty of art, like all beauty, not only tells of the nature of our final horizon and goal but also evokes its gratuitous presence, drawing us to that goal and giving us already the taste of its reality.[5]

Unfortunately, as he observes, Roman Catholic theology since Trent has been largely dominated by a philosophical and conceptual approach. "Paul Tillich was correct, however, in seeing in such 'philosophical' theology a secondary and derivative specialization: the primary language of theology (like that of religion) is symbolic."[6]

The late Andrew Greeley frequently made the same point; he stressed repeatedly that Catholicism was passed on most effectively, not by its "high tradition," the cognitive, propositional, didactic teaching of theologians and the magisterium, but by its "popular tradition," the stories of parents, family, neighbors, and friends. Think of the stories you learned as a child that still shape your religious imagination. The high tradition represents a prosaic Catholicism; popular tradition is poetic.[7] Both are necessary.

Beauty

But how much more powerful is that affective, imaginative dimension of Catholicism, its appreciation of beauty natural and created, sacramental or ritual, in symbol, music, or song? Beauty can open us to the mystery of God.

> Christ plays in ten thousand places,
> Lovely in limbs, and lovely in eyes not his.

> —Gerard Manley Hopkins
> "As kingfishers catch fire,
> dragonflies dráw flame"

3

SILENCE

They say silence is golden. Perhaps that is because it is so rare. We live in a world of noise. The extraversion of contemporary life, with music, television, and the constant intrusiveness of the advertising industry, leaves little room for silence. Young people, especially, are surrounded by electronically mediated conversations, sounds, and images. Stimulation is constant. Campus dorms pulse with sounds from competing stereos. Knowledge comes from liquid crystal screens, not books. Students walk alone but always talking on cell phones or checking e-mail.

SILENCE AND GOD

Dominican University's William George calls for a greater emphasis on solitude in undergraduate education. "When solitude does not degenerate into an isolating 'iPodism,' students may come face to face with themselves, not only with their capacity to wonder, which reaches toward the divine, but also with their self-deceits and penchant for sham."[1] Similarly, Cardinal Carlo Martini once wrote, "We need to move away from an unhealthy slavery to rumors and endless chattering, from characterless music that only makes noise, and find each day at least one half-hour of silence and a half-day each week to think about ourselves, to reflect and pray for a longer period." He says that may be difficult for many, but young people, when offered an experience of interior peace and tranquility on a retreat, "take courage and find it to be an unprecedented source of life and joy."[2]

Often in driving onto the grounds of our former novitiate at the foot of the mountains in Santa Barbara, or past the gate of my favorite monastery to begin my annual retreat, I've experienced the sudden silence as something tangible. I can feel myself relax, as though a physical burden has been lifted from my shoulders. To enter into the silence is to enter into prayer. At the ecumenical monastery of Taizé in France's beautiful Burgundy region, as the guests assemble for the prayer in the Church of Reconciliation, young people stand before the doors with signs that read simply, "Silence." For it is in silence that we encounter the mysterious Divine Presence. Meister Eckhart says, "Nothing in all creation is so like God as stillness." And Thomas Merton: "The inspirations of the Holy Ghost are quiet, for God speaks in the silent depths of the spirit. His voice brings peace."[3]

Perhaps my closest experience of this mystery is walking the long mile and a half through the fields and orchards at a Trappist monastery when making my retreat. The road runs straight across a great valley. Above, the sky is brilliant blue, with a few white clouds and crossed by contrails from jets high overhead; the fields and orchards are deep green with golden wheat flowing like an ocean. The overwhelming impression is one of vastness, space, openness, with the fields stretching on either side to the mountains, some of them snowcapped, which border the valley. You can smell the plowed earth, feel the warm sun, hear the breeze in your ears, and sense the presence of the God of silence, the God whose very silence is speech. It's hard to describe the feeling. I want to expand my heart, take it all in, somehow become one with it. I feel my spirit completely at peace, deeply content, yet full of longing, with a sense that I cannot get enough. Brian McDermott speaks of "that place of ultimate emptiness and longing which is our transcendence, our creatureliness, where only God (or sin, as the power which tries to undo God's presence) can be present."[4]

SILENCE AND PRAYER

The long tradition of monasticism in both the Eastern and Western churches is testimony to how silence can nourish a life of prayer. For Merton, a person unable to live with silence was not ready for the monastic life. He wrote, "The immature person, when forced to be silent, tends to experience his inauthenticity and has no escape from it. Communication with others, even about nothing, at least offers some diversion."[5] It is interesting that some contemporary contemplative communities, already committed to long periods of silence, schedule weekly "desert days" for their members so that, freed from normal routines and duties, they can experience an even greater solitude and silence.

We need to encourage people to become comfortable with prayer and retreat experiences that privilege silence. In accompanying students on a silent Ignatian retreat, I've often found them slightly apprehensive at the beginning. Meals in silence? No talking? Put away my cell phone? No way! But once they enter into the retreat experience, they begin to relax and enjoy it. Their sensitivity is enhanced. They become aware of things they otherwise would miss, and soon discover a new sense of community with their fellow retreatants. Some seek quiet time in the chapel; others take long walks in which they begin to experience nature in a new way. They find themselves with a new care for each other. They are opening up to mystery.

This new experience of silent prayer explains in part the attraction for eucharistic adoration on many of our campuses today. Many young people long for an experience of the holy. They don't always find it at our too-often-chatty liturgies. The holy is lost in noise. In its presence, the proper attitude is reverence, and indeed, silence. Recall Moses before the burning bush: "Remove the sandals from your feet, for the place on which you are standing is holy ground" (Exod 3:5).

Pope Benedict called repeatedly for greater reverence and more silence in the liturgy. An overemphasis on the Eucharist as a communal meal or "celebration" has led to a loss of its sacred and sacrificial dimensions. Too often, our liturgies have become overly wordy, didactic, and even banal. If the liturgical experimentation of the seventies and early eighties is behind us, the language of lectors and presiders at least in the United States usually focuses on celebration, community, ministry, and hospitality, with far less attention to entering into the holy or approaching the altar of God as we once prayed. The horizontal has replaced the vertical. Those coming from a highly sensate culture, overstimulated, constantly talking or texting on cell phones, choosing from the hundreds of songs on their iPods, or from a world of images only a mouse click away, are accustomed to being in control. As someone once commented, "If you have an iPod, you don't need to listen to any song you don't love."

Thus, many from this generation have lost a sense for worship. They tire easily of repeated liturgical formulas and familiar eucharistic prayers. Ritual no longer satisfies. They want variety. As Joseph Ratzinger wrote:

> This is why, here especially, we are in such an urgent need of an education toward inwardness. We need to be taught to enter into the heart of things. As far as liturgy is concerned, this is a matter of life or death. The only way we can be saved from succumbing to the inflation of words is if we have the courage to face silence and in it learn to listen afresh to *the Word*. Otherwise we shall be overwhelmed by "mere words" at the very point where we should be encountering the Word, the Logos, the Word of love, crucified and risen, who brings us life and joy.[6]

THE GOD WHO SPEAKS IN SILENCE

It is in silence that God speaks. God is beyond image and sound, but we often sense God's mysterious presence in silence. It is comforting, sustaining, and life-giving. It brings a deep sense of peace. We know that we have been touched, that we are not alone. Nature, especially, speaks of God, brings God near. But the very taste of God awakens a deeper hunger, a desire for more, for some way to move beyond the veil, to see God's face. St. Catherine of Siena, doctor of the church, captures beautifully this experience of the Divine Mystery:

> It is the experience of God who cannot be known directly but in drawing near awakens in us a hunger that can never be stilled, a desire that can never be satisfied. You are a mystery as deep as the sea; the more I search, the more I find, and the more I find the more I search for you. But I can never be satisfied; what I receive will ever leave me desiring more. When you fill my soul I have an even greater hunger and I grow more famished for your light.[7]

The Son's presence is more challenging. Jesus is not a culturally constructed friend but a person with a real history. We know him from the Gospels; we are familiar with his words and strive to make them our own. Thus, he has a voice. But his words are not always comforting. He calls us, makes demands, and invites us to follow him. He tells us we must lose our life to save it, that the last shall be first, that we must carry our cross with him, and that we can embrace him in the poor.

Christ also has a body, both sacramental and ecclesial. To be "in Christ"—a phrase that appears 164 times in Paul's letters—should not be understood in an exclusively individual sense as it often is today. Being in Christ "does not mean a purely individual relationship between Christ and the believer. It means belonging to the realm within which Christ rules, and that realm is his body, the community."[8] Thus, the phrase is primarily ecclesiological. For Paul, the unity of the Church is affected through baptism and the Eucharist, what the later Church would call its sacraments. Baptism breaks down barriers of race, ethnicity, social status, and gender (1 Cor 12:13; Gal 3:27–29; cf. Rom 10:12; Eph 2:14–16). The Eucharist unites the baptized into the one Body of Christ in their communion in his body and blood (1 Cor 10:16–17).

The Spirit's presence is more subtle, more affect than object. The Spirit personifies God's creative presence, hovering over the waters of chaos at Creation, inspiring the prophets, leading Jesus into the desert, and empowering his ministry. We recognize the Spirit's presence reflexively in our interior lives. The Spirit inspires, animates, and breathes within us. It is the living source of our faith. We are convinced that God is real, that we can call on God as Abba (Rom 8:15), confess Jesus as Lord (1 Cor 12:3), and know that our sins have been forgiven (Rom 6:20–23).

We experience the "fruit of the Spirit" in love, joy, patience, kindness, generosity, faithfulness, gentleness, and self-control (Gal 5:22–23). We are drawn by the Spirit in love, the greatest of the Spirit's gifts (1 Cor 13:13), toward the God we cannot see, and find a communion with others who have come to new life in Christ.

The Gospels show us Jesus seeking out time for silence and solitude. Much of his life was spent in the silence of Nazareth, working as a carpenter, most probably alone. After the experience at his baptism, he retired to the desert for a period of prayer and reflection, and he experienced temptation. His public life began after his return from the desert. But he continued to seek solitude. Often he rose early in the morning for prayer by himself or withdrew from his disciples to be alone. Out of this silence grew his intimacy with the one he called Abba, who empowered his ministry.

> It doesn't have to be
> the blue iris, it could be
> weeds in a vacant lot, or a few
> small stones; just
> pay attention, then patch

a few words together and don't try
to make them elaborate, this isn't
a contest but the doorway

into thanks, and a silence in which
another voice may speak.

—Mary Oliver, "Praying"

4

EVIL

Recently, National Public Radio's *Morning Edition* did a weeklong series of interviews of unchurched young adults under thirty. Their reasons for remaining unaffiliated or for leaving their churches tended to fall into a number of classic objections to faith, such as an inability to understand the symbols and stories of their religious tradition, a perceived conflict between religion and science, and disagreement with church teachings. But most frequently mentioned was the problem of evil and suffering.

EVIL AND TRAGEDY

Evil is most devastating when it is personal. This was evident in a number of respondents referring to the disillusionment of trying to deal with personal tragedy. They spoke of praying and having nothing happen, wondering why God didn't answer their prayers. One recounted the death of an only son, the victim of gun violence at the age of twenty-one, asking what kind of God lets a child be shot. Another found the story of God asking Abraham to sacrifice his son Isaac incredible, saying that anyone making such a request should be locked up: "There's no way that this happened. I wasn't buying it."

In his great play *J.B.*, a modern retelling of the story of the biblical figure Job, Archibald MacLeish cries out, "If God is good He is not God. If God is God He is not good." Perhaps the classic statement is Ivan Karamazov's protest against the suffering of innocent children in Dostoyevsky's great novel *The Brothers Karamazov*. After reciting a long list of children tortured and murdered, he tells the story of the eight-year-old son of a serf who accidently injures his master's favorite dog with a stone. The master, a general, orders the child stripped naked, forces him to run, and sets his dogs upon him, who tear the child to pieces. Ivan, the righteous atheist, rejects God's salvation, arguing that it "is not worth the tears of that one tortured child."

It needs to be said at the beginning that suffering, tragedy, and evil are mysteries beyond our ability to understand. Our beautiful world is imperfect. It is not some kind of machine, operating according to inflexible "natural" laws, but a complex set of relationships based on the probabilities that lie at the heart of nature. Sometimes things go wrong: normal development is impaired, cancers develop, tectonic plates shift, atmospheric anomalies produce devastating storms. Humankind too has not cast off completely the predatory nature of its evolutionary history and must continually be called to a higher purpose. Freedom, reflecting our creation in the divine image (Gen 1:27), means freedom for good but also freedom for evil, and sometimes evil seems to triumph.

A SELF-EFFACING GOD

A universe of freedom means a self-limitation of the divine power. Jesus shows us a God who has absolutely renounced violence, a self-effacing God who, for our sake, has become powerless. In one of his most powerful statements about the universe, Pope John Paul II said that "in a certain sense one could say that *confronted with our human freedom, God decided to make Himself 'impotent.'*"[1] God is not the author of evil. This also means that God cannot step in to "set things right" whenever something goes wrong. The world has its own causality. Similarly, John Haught speaks of a God who suffers along with creation, revealing the theme of divine suffering love.[2] But God is not absent from creation.

One of my favorite spiritual writers is Etty Hillesum, a young Jewish woman who lived in Amsterdam during World War II. She began as a gifted but rather self-absorbed girl, secular in her upbringing, not a person of faith. As a young woman, she went through several affairs, but as she lived through the tragedy of her Jewish people caught up in the Holocaust, she developed a mystic's sense of God's presence. Convinced of God's reality in the midst of terror, she ministered to Dutch Jews at a transit camp called Westerbork, trying to comfort them and provide for their needs before that terrible journey to the east.

Her diary, *An Interrupted Life*, was only published long after the war. In it she rejoiced to be "at the center of all human suffering." She spoke about her desire to help God, even feeling a compassion for God, a strange expression, but one I've read in other mystics and masters of the spiritual life:

> I shall try to help You, God, to stop my strength ebbing away.... But one thing is becoming increasingly clear to me: that You cannot help us, that we must help You to help ourselves.... all that really matters: that we safeguard the little piece of You, God, in ourselves.... I shall always labor for You and remain faithful to You and I shall never drive You from my presence."[3]

Etty's story is of a God who is always with us, but who is in some mysterious way dependent on us, calling forth what is best in us. Her diary ends with the words, "We should be willing to act as a balm for all wounds." She died at Auschwitz in 1943. Thus God is not the cause of evil; rather God is always at work, bringing good out of evil, victory out of defeat, life out of death. Blaming God is too simple; it reflects a commonsense theology, not one rooted in the Jewish or Christian tradition.

Still, it is true that evil often triumphs because of human sinfulness. Pope Benedict XVI has long been skeptical about the possibilities of justice in a world that is fallen, and stresses the fragile character of human freedom, no doubt influenced by his experience of coming of age under the horrors of Hitler's Third Reich. In his encyclical on hope, *Spe salvi*, he argued that freedom always remains freedom for evil (no. 21). We place ourselves and our own concerns first. Closed to grace, we act out of unhealed psychological wounds, peer pressure, or race or class prejudice. We can be small-minded, dishonest, and mean-spirited.

Sometimes we are shaped by external factors. A dysfunctional family background, poverty, violence, or abuse can deafen one to the quiet voice of God within. Our cultures can embody fear of change, an exaggerated sense of wrong, hatred for those who are different, or a simple lack of respect for others. One has only to look around to see so many victims of poverty, injustice, or violence.

The twentieth century has seen numerous genocides, two world wars, and the destructive power of atomic weapons. International terrorism is a new threat. Countries like Egypt, Iraq, Syria, Iran, Pakistan, Sudan, and India have been torn by religious violence, done by some in the name of God. Many in their populations are desperately poor, with little opportunities for education and a better life. Some of these countries seem incapable of democracy. Millions have become refugees, seeking a better life for their families or simply safety from violence. In India, China, and Pakistan, a preference for sons leads to the abortion of thousands of female fetuses, leading to a serious imbalance between males and females in the general population. In the Republic of the Congo, perhaps as many as 400,000 women have been raped and mutilated; some estimate a thousand rapes a day. In many African countries, children have been kidnapped, the boys to serve as child soldiers and the girls to be used for sexual purposes. Young girls undergo often permanently damaging female circumcision. Closer to home, in the United States today, 16 percent of the population lives in poverty, 20 percent of them children. Many still lack health care. A little more than half a million people are homeless. Gun-related deaths are eight times higher than in countries that are politically and economically similar to the United States.

EVIL DOES NOT HAVE THE LAST WORD

With so much tragedy, violence, and suffering, it is easy to see why some find it difficult to believe in a good God. As Walter Kasper says, "Suffering in the world is clearly modern atheism's weightiest argument."[4] But nowhere is the apparent triumph of evil more evident than in the story of Jesus, God's only beloved Son. Raised in a traditional Jewish home, nourished by the sacred texts of his people, religiously observant (cf. Luke 4:16–22), Jesus gradually discerned a calling to proclaim the nearness of God's salvation, the kingdom of God, particularly after his encounter with John the Baptist at the Jordan.

Gathering a group of men and women around him, some of them from the company of the Baptist, his disciples formed what scholars today call the "Jesus movement." Jesus himself used the metaphor of a new family consisting of those who do the will of God (Mark 3:31–35). He spent his short life reaching out to others, speaking of God's nearness, healing the sick, setting free those troubled by oppressive spirits, reconciling the outcast, and preaching the good news to the poor. But as so often happens, his goodness aroused fierce opposition.

Perhaps it was his action in the temple, driving out the buyers and sellers that led the authorities to decide on his death. This was more than an act of outraged piety, concerned for the sanctity of his Father's house. In driving out those who sold small animals and made change for financial transactions, Jesus was effectively shutting down the temple cult, saying with a prophetic gesture that the time of the temple was past. The religious authorities had not recognized God's message in his preaching. This they could not tolerate; so they conspired with the Romans to bring about his death.

The story of Jesus tells us that God is not unaware of our pain. Perhaps this is the only answer to the woman who asks about a God who allows a child to be shot. God has been there. As Isaiah said, fore-shadowing the sufferings of the Servant of Yahweh:

> I gave my back to those who struck me,
> and my cheeks to those who pulled out the beard;
> I did not hide my face
> from insult and spitting.
>
> (Isa 50:6)

Jesus has felt abandonment, humiliation, and abuse. He experienced the sting of injustice. Was it to pay for our sins, as though God demanded this suffering as the price of our redemption? No, Jesus's passion was brought on by the opposition his preaching raised. He became the target for the self-interest, anger, and violence that are the expression of evil and sin. He took that violence on himself. It was precisely in being faithful to his mission that he died.

Was he tempted to rage, strike out, to answer violence with violence, even to despair? He must have been; he entered fully into our humanity and was well aware of its limitations. He felt abandoned by God. But he remained faithful even unto death, clinging to the one he called Abba, forgiving those who abused him, and offering hope to the thief crucified beside him. And God did not let go of him. God raised him up to life, for God's love is stronger than death. Evil does not have the last word.

5

HOPE

Hope is an elusive virtue. It reaches beyond the present with its struggles, disappointments, and pain to put us in touch with a richer tomorrow; it suggests that we are not alone, that the future is bright with promise, that our yearnings will be fulfilled, and that our desire for love will be realized with a security that embraces us. Ultimately, hope is personal; it presumes a loving, personal presence, a Thou, a God of justice and love who heals our wounds, holds us close, and will not let go. Hope is thus transformative; it promises a fulfillment beyond our ability to imagine.

THE GIFT OF HOPE

But hope is a gift; not all have it, or are able to hope. The life of Virginia Woolf, the famous English writer raised in privilege by her free-thinking parents, was marked by tragedy. Scarred by sexual abuse by her two half brothers when she was six and the early loss of her parents, she was unbending in her atheism, a stance typical of many intellectuals in the Britain of the 1920s. When she heard that T.S. Eliot had come to faith, she reportedly wrote to a friend, "I have had a most shameful and distressing interview with dear Tom Eliot, who may be called dead to us all from this day forward. He has become an Anglo-Catholic believer in God and immortality, and goes to church. I was shocked. A corpse would seem to me more credible than he is. I mean, there's something obscene in a living person sitting by the fire and believing in God."[1]

If true, there is something rather defensive in her remarks. She protests too much. Why should another person's openness to the mystery of the divine be offensive, end a relationship, or be so unsettling? Perhaps it speaks to the emptiness in her life, even a longing for something more. Certainly she was not happy. Despite her success as a writer, Woolf suffered from mood swings and depression. She found little to hope in. In March 1941, she filled her pockets with stones and waded into the River Ouse, taking her life.

The story of Dag Hammarskjöld, the Swedish economist and diplomat, is quite different. A public servant for most of his life and Secretary-General of the United Nations (1953–61), he died on September 18, 1961, in Northern Rhodesia, now Zambia, in a suspicious plane crash. In his spiritual diary, he had written, "God does not die on the day when we cease to believe in a personal deity, but we die on the day when our lives cease to be illuminated by the steady radiance, renewed daily, of a wonder, the source of which is beyond all reason."[2] A "steady radiance," a lovely way to describe God's mysterious presence in our lives, the presence we have to renew or nourish even if we cannot fully comprehend it. But God's presence makes itself felt; it comforts and illumines, calling us from the present into a future only vaguely glimpsed. That presence gives us hope.

In the Old Testament, hope in God's faithfulness is a constant. The psalms of lament, for example, hold out hope that God will rescue and redeem those that cry out to him, often expressed in the final verses in what scholars call a "certainty of hearing" (Pss 6; 22; 31; 57). In the midst of his troubles, Job exclaims, "I know that my Redeemer lives.... [and] in my flesh I shall see God" (Job 19:25–26). According to the very late Book of Wisdom, "The souls of the righteous are in the hand of God, and no torment will ever touch them" (Wis 3:1). In the Gospels, Jesus tells us we are not alone, that the God who feeds the birds and clothes the lilies of the field in a glory greater than that of Solomon cares for us even more (cf. Matt 6:25–34), that God who gave his only Son out of love for the world (John 3:16) will give the Holy Spirit to those who ask (Luke 11:13). As he takes leave of his disciples in his last discourse, Jesus tells them, "I go to prepare a place for you … [and] I will come again and will take you to myself, so that where I am, there you may also be" (John 14:2–3).

POPE BENEDICT ON HOPE

In his encyclical on hope, *Spe salvi*, Pope Benedict XVI speaks of the virtue of hope as reassuring the early Christians that their lives would not end in emptiness, even if they did not know the details of what awaited them. This hope was life-changing. "The dark door of time, of the future, has been thrown open. Whoever has hope lives differently; the one who hopes has been granted the gift of a new life" (no. 2). He cites the Letter to the Hebrews, which links hope with faith: "Faith is the assurance of things hoped for, the conviction of things not seen" (Heb 11:1).

He goes on to argue that, in Western culture, Christian hope has largely been lost, or more accurately, under the influence of the scientific revolution, the French Revolution, and the Enlightenment, it has been secularized. Salvation, no longer union with a loving God, has been reduced to belief in progress based on science. Freed from the shackles of faith, doctrine, and the Church, reason has emerged as autonomous and free, with human beings left to determine for themselves what is true, good, and beautiful. The kingdom of God is downgraded to a human reality, not God's transforming presence. At the same time, a scientific materialism has reduced our beautiful universe to mindless bits of matter, without purpose, governed by the laws of probability and random evolution; what remains is a cold cosmos of vast distances, black holes, and dying stars. It is empty of spirit.

Benedict turns especially to Marx, whose concern for the work-ing poor held up a new eschatological vision of a classless society in which all was shared and each received what was necessary. Benedict's analysis of modernity's thinkers with their reduction of the kingdom of God to an earthly reality is surprisingly respectful, but he argues that their worldview was doomed from the start because it ignores the ambiguous character of human freedom and the reality of sin. Freedom, he writes, always remains freedom for evil. Marx thought that once the economy had been put right, justice and peace would prevail. A beautiful thought, if naïve. His real error was his materialism: human beings, in fact, are not merely the product of economic conditions, and it is not possible to redeem them purely from the outside by creating a favorable economic environment. When the revolution came, what it left behind was "a trail of appalling destruction" (*Spe salvi* 21).

Indeed, as the postmodernists point out, the twentieth century brought not utopia but innumerable genocides, two world wars, the horror of nuclear weapons, terrorism, and a growing divide between the wealthy and the very poor. Benedict, having grown up in Hitler's Germany, is well aware of the bankruptcy of modernity's blind trust in material progress. He quotes Theodor Adorno of the Frankfurt School, known for its critique of modernity; Adorno described faith in technical progress without progress in ethics and morality as progress "from the sling to the atom bomb" (no. 22). So much for an uncritical faith in progress!

Nor has faith been left untouched by "the acids of modernity." For many people of faith today, hope has been reduced to an individualistic doctrine of salvation, a "born again" theology that promises heaven to the individual and leaves the world to its misery. Many fundamentalist churches in Asia, Africa, and Latin America subscribe to the "Prosperity Gospel," promising wealth and success to those Christians who give their lives to Jesus. Others look forward to the Rapture, when God lifts the saved out of this vale of tears, with the others "left behind." Benedict turns to the fathers of the Church to show how salvation has always been considered a "social reality." We come to salvation only through charity, by being linked "to a lived union with a 'people,' and for each individual it can only be attained within this 'we'" (*Spe salvi* 14). We come to salvation within this plurality.

Our lives are inescapably linked to those of others, from the moment of our conception through the multitude of relationships that shape us, whether familial, social, or cultural, making us the persons we become, and through which we touch and shape others, for better or worse. Faith and ethics are inseparable, for relationships are real, transformative; we do not come to heaven as monads but always linked to others whom we have helped or hindered along the way. It is not science that redeems us, but God's love. Genuine love helps us understand this. When someone has the experience of a great love, this is a graced moment of "redemption" that gives a new meaning to life. We need a love that is unconditional, that sense that "neither death, nor life, nor angels, nor rulers, nor things present, nor things to come, nor powers, nor height, nor depth, nor anything else in all creation, will be able to separate us from the love of God in Christ Jesus our Lord" (Rom 8:38–39).

ESCHATOLOGICAL HOPE

This is hope. More than material, it is eschatological. It includes God's justice for all those who have suffered injustice, all the victims of history. Benedict insists that grace does not cancel out justice. He cites Dostoyevsky, who in *The Brothers Karamazov* wrote that "evildoers, in the end, do not sit at table at the eternal banquet beside their victims without distinction, as though nothing had happened" (*Spe salvi* 44). Christian hope looks forward to the day when God will dwell with his people, wiping away the tears from their eyes, and mourning and crying, death and pain will be no more (cf. Rev 21:3–4).

The final scene in James Cameron's film *Titanic* is wonderfully suggestive. Rose DeWitt-Bukater, now a one-hundred-year-old Rose Dawson Calvert, is with her granddaughter on a research vessel probing the wreck of the Titanic for a necklace with a huge diamond called "the Heart of the Ocean." The search is unsuccessful, but Rose, who found the necklace in her overcoat after that terrible night in 1912 when the great ship struck the iceberg, gets up at night, walks to the stern of the ship, and drops the necklace into the deep.

She returns to her bed, and as she slips away in a dream or more probably from old age, she revisits those days long ago on the Titanic; she imagines passing through the ship's great promenade, now in the wreckage on the ocean floor, filled with the debris. As the promenade is magically transformed, the dark blue light of the deep turning to the brilliance of the once great ship, she enters the ship's Grand Staircase, where those she once knew greet her with applause. On the stairs, she is reunited with the young man who on that tragic night saved her life, her beloved Jack. Yes, a Hollywood ending, but it also suggests a love that endures, a love that takes us beyond the tragedies and loss of this life to another where there is fulfillment and joy. This is God's love.

Recently, I read of a conversation between a pastor and an atheist. The pastor said, "One day, I was talking to an atheist, a young man who told me, 'I don't believe in God.' 'That's okay,' the pastor responded, 'God still believes in you.'"

> My Lord God, I have no idea where I am going. I do not see the road ahead of me. I cannot know for certain where it will end. Nor do I really know myself, and the fact that I think that I am following your will does not mean that I am actually doing so. But I believe that the desire to please you does in fact please you. And I hope I have that desire in all that I am doing. I hope that I will never do anything apart from that desire. And I know that if I do this you will lead me by the right road though I may know nothing about it. Therefore will I trust you always though I may seem to be lost and in the shadow of death. I will not fear, for you are ever with me, and you will never leave me to face my perils alone. Amen.
>
> —prayer of Thomas Merton

6

A Love That Endures

HBO's show *Girls*, Lena Dunham's comedy-drama about four mid-twenties young women living on their own in New York, is more than just another HBO show with lots of drama, nudity, and sharp dialogue. Still girls, really, the young women in the drama bounce in and out of relationships, some of them abusive; marry suddenly and just as suddenly divorce; visit an abortion clinic; lose roommates after emotional fights; worry about where the next check is coming from; laugh and party a lot; but seem unable to share any personal feelings. Underneath it all, they are desperately lonely. They are seeking love in all the wrong places. After several failed affairs, Hanna, the main character (played by Dunham), cries out, "I just want someone who wants to hang out all the time and thinks I'm the best person in the world and wants to have sex with only me."

LOVE AND COMMITMENT

They are not the only lonely people in the world today. There are millions of them, especially in our fast-paced, secular Western cultures. Recent studies show that at the majority of colleges and universities today, women outnumber men by a ratio of 60 to 40. The gender ratio in 2013 was 57 to 43. Where this is the case, women are at a disadvantage. Male-female relationships on campuses where men outnumber the women often emphasize courtship and monogamy. However, an overabundance of women on campus can show a decrease in healthy relationships. These colleges and universities often struggle to deal with date rape, which leaves young women feeling powerless and victimized.[1] A former student of mine with great courage described in the student newspaper how this had happened to her. Too often, dating in the traditional sense has been replaced by "hooking up," sex without relationship, intimacy without commitment. One study in the *Journal of Sex Research* reports that college women are twice as likely as college men to experience distress after hookups.[2] How sad, when the beauty of sexual intimacy and love, in which each gives oneself to the other, has been reduced to a brief overnight encounter. Bob Dylan expressed this in a tragic song made popular by Joan Baez, a song about broken relationships built around the refrain, "Love is Just a Four Letter Word."[3] The result is not couples bonded by a deep love but broken hearts, jaded lives, and often sexually transmitted diseases (STDs).

So who loves you? Echoing Lena Dunham, is there someone who thinks you are the best person in the world? Is it a parent or grandparent, a spouse, sibling, boyfriend or girlfriend, or just a dear friend? Do your relationships nourish or drain you? Are you like the song—looking for love in all the wrong places? Is there someone who will always be there for you, whose love is unending?

You know how you feel when someone truly loves you, when you see it in their eyes. That loving glance that changes the way you feel about yourself; it is transformative. When I think about love, I remember my parents, in their great love for each other. Their marriage is one of the greatest gifts that I have received. My siblings and I grew up secure in their love for each other, in the family they created, the home they made. I can still see them cuddling in the kitchen in their late seventies, embarrassing us kids.

True love is enduring; it lasts through time and challenge. Dorothy Day deeply loved her former common-law husband, Forster Batterham, but being the anarchist that he was, he could accept neither the institution of marriage nor her Catholic faith. Forced to choose, Dorothy chose her faith and they separated. But generally unknown until very recently with the publication of some of her letters was that they kept in touch over the years with notes, gifts, and hospital visits. In her final years, Forster called her daily, and he was present at her funeral. She considered his love a graced moment in her life; according to Robert Ellsberg, she said, "It was because through a whole love, both physical and spiritual, I came to know God."[4]

Those in the Marriage Encounter movement like to say that love is a decision, not a feeling. In his *Spiritual Exercises*, St. Ignatius of Loyola says that love is expressed in deeds. But too often we forget that we are called to love each other.

TRUE LOVE

There is one who loves you faithfully, the God who formed your inmost being, who knit you together in your mother's womb (cf. Ps 139:13). The God who promises to always be with you, "because you are precious in my sight, and honored, and I love you" (Isa 43:4), who says that even if your mother should forget you, he will never forget you, for he has written your name upon the palms of his hands (Isa 49:15–16). That is God's love, and it is truly transformative.

I remember years ago, after a visit to Taizé in France, three of us stopped at a cloistered Carmelite convent on the way home. It was February, a drizzly day, cold and grey. The out sister led us into a parlor, where a fire burned in the grate. Three young sisters came in to visit with us, three of the most alive, beautiful women I think I have ever met. Their eyes were bright, their faces radiant, glowing. They sat quietly, their brown habits draped gracefully around them, but full of life as we chatted. These were women in love with God, and it showed. Later, as we continued our journey, a young German Lutheran in our group, preparing for ordination, was confused by their way of life. "But what do they do?" he kept asking as we continued our journey. "What is their work?" He couldn't understand a life devoted simply to prayer and contemplation.

In his first encyclical, *Deus caritas est*, Pope Benedict XVI described God as both reason and love. "God is the absolute and ultimate source of all being," he wrote, "but this universal principle of creation—the *Logos*, primordial reason—is at the same time a lover with all the passion of a true love" (no. 10). In a world in which the name of God is sometimes associated with hatred and violence, as he notes in the introduction to the encyclical, Benedict writes to assure us of God's passionate love, poured out upon us, which we are in turn to share with others.

This most sober of scholars goes on to describe the love that is God as including both *eros* and *agape*, for he sees love as a single reality with different dimensions. *Eros* is that profound desire that draws one person to another, with its suggestion of the physical and the sexual, as in the word *erotic*. He refers to the "boldly erotic images" used by the prophets to describe God's passion for his people, the metaphors of betrothal and marriage. Idolatry, the worship of other gods, is thus adultery or prostitution (no. 9). *Agape* is that unselfish love that seeks first the good of the beloved, even at the cost of renunciation and sacrifice. This divine activity takes on dramatic form when, in Jesus Christ, it is God himself who goes in search of lost humanity (no. 12). Thus this God is not a distant God, a divine architect whose work is done, but a God active through Word and Spirit, creating, sustaining, and drawing toward himself.

The mystery of the Trinity is at the very center of Christian faith, disclosing for us something of the Divine Mystery. It assures us that relationality is at the very heart of God. God is Father, Son, and Spirit, a communion of person, equal in majesty, one in being. As Michael Downey says, "The term 'person' when used of God is a way of saying that God is always toward and for the other in the self-giving which is constitutive of love. Self-giving is always in relation to another, to others."[5] God's love is a gift, poured out through the Word to create and redeem and to bring creation back to its fulfillment in the Divine Mystery in the Spirit "so that God may be all in all" (1 Cor 15:28).

In speaking of "God's passionate love for his people" (no. 10), Benedict reclaims the power of *eros* for Christian theology. For while an undisciplined *eros* reduces love to the physical—to sex, even to a commodification of the object of our desire—true *eros* leads us beyond ourselves, toward infinity, eternity, the Divine (no. 5). The pope is so insightful here. That powerful erotic energy, which too often we dismiss as something lustful or evil, leading us into sin, really speaks of God's desire for us and the mysterious ways we are drawn toward the transcendent, toward God.

Often we can experience this attractive power of *eros*. The beauty of a child's face, a glowing sunset or star-filled sky, a great work of art, a teenager's glowing complexion, an oak tree spreading its branches, Beethoven's *Eroica*—any of these can pull us out of ourselves. Similarly, we can be moved by an act of graciousness or generosity or forgiveness, even a scene in a film. Our eyes fill with tears, we feel awe, even something visceral. In our bodies, we are sensing the existence or goodness itself, or of absolute beauty, already mysteriously apprehended, something beyond but real. It is the pull of the divine.

Thus our deepest desires are spiritual; *eros* puts us in touch with the transcendent. St. Augustine asks, What does the soul desire more than truth? He speaks of this desire as a hunger of our "spiritual palate" for wisdom, justice, truth, and eternal life.[6] *"You have made us for yourself, O Lord, and our hearts are restless until they find their rest in you."*[7] If God cannot be directly known, we are drawn toward the true, the good, and the beautiful that reflect the divine fullness of being. But we do not always attend to these desires. The philosopher Martin Heidegger once spoke about a "forgetfulness of being" (*Seinvergessenheit*), meaning that we too often neglect to ask that fundamental metaphysical question, Why is there anything at all?[8] We have forgotten our origin in the mystery that is love.

Too often we shut ourselves off from God's love. When we let it in, it is transformative. It can open us to others, gentling our hard hearts and giving us hearts of flesh. Dorothy Day writes about a graced moment in her own life when she experienced God's love. She was riding home after a meeting in Brooklyn, sitting opposite a few poor people on a bus.

> One of them, a downcast, ragged man, suddenly epitomized for me the desolation, the hopelessness of the destitute, and I began to weep. I had been struck by one of those "beams of love," wounded by it in a most particular way. It was my own condition that I was weeping about—my own hardness of heart, my own sinfulness.[9]

If Dunham's character in the HBO drama is desperately lonely beyond all her sexual adventures, God's love is everlasting. Not even death can break that bond. This is the great lesson of the story of Jesus. This is the joy of the gospel.

PART II
JESUS

7

INCARNATION

And the Word became flesh and lived among us.

—John 1:14

In the Prologue to John's Gospel, the author says, "The Word became flesh and lived among us." In the original Greek, the language is more vivid. The line reads literally, "The Word became flesh and pitched his tent among us." This is John's way of saying that in Jesus, God entered fully into our lives, became one of us, and lived among us. The Prologue served as the original reading for the Church's liturgical celebration of the birth of Jesus, before it was eclipsed by Luke's nativity story. What John is telling us is that we find God in the human. Or as Cardinal Avery Dulles once said, "The Incarnation does not provide us a ladder by which to escape the ambiguities of life and scale the heights of heaven. Rather the Incarnation enables us to burrow deep into the heart of planet Earth and find it shimmering with divinity."[1]

It's easy to sentimentalize the Christmas story: a newborn babe in a stable, watched by his parents, warmed by the breath of the animals, and visited by shepherds. Around our mangers are red poinsettias, evergreen trees draped with light, and Christmas carols. We enter into the joy of the season by exchanging cards with family and friends one hasn't seen in ages. We try to reach out, make some contact, share a little of our lives, and learn something of theirs. With the good news, there is also so much sorrow, pain, and tragedy. People have died, dear friends struggle with cancer or other debilitating diseases, marriages have ended, people have lost jobs, and others face new disappointments. This is the world into which God has chosen to come.

AN IGNATIAN VISION

In his *Spiritual Exercises*, St. Ignatius invites the retreatant through a contemplation on the incarnation to imagine the Trinity looking down over the Earth, seeing people in such great diversity in dress and manner of acting. Some are white, some black; some at peace, and some at war; some are weeping, others laughing. Some are well, some sick; some are coming into the world, some dying. The language is somewhat naïve, but Ignatius is trying to evoke a humanity in need of God's healing touch. Still, at its heart, the story is true. The eternal Word of God took on flesh in the child born to a poor couple, sheltering in an insignificant village, to offer us a share in the divine life.

When I think of the world, there is so much pain, suffering, injustice: hunger in Somalia and Sudan; violence against women in India or the Congo or Mexico; a diminishing Christian presence in the Arab world. More Christians suffer violence and death today than at any moment in history, and they are not the only ones who suffer religious oppression. There are new examples of racism, violence, and the persecution of minorities and others who are different. The early decades of the twenty-first century have seen millions on the move: refugees from violence in their home countries—sometimes religiously based, often from wars that do not seem to end—seeking safety for their families and a decent life. Others live in modern-day slavery. Estimates put the number at 20.9 million—78 percent for labor, 22 percent for sex, 55 percent of them women and girls. Terrorists kill hundreds with airport attacks and car bombs. This is the world into which God comes. This is the deeper meaning of the incarnation, of Christmas.

In Jesus, God came to be part of this world, but not all welcomed him. "He came to what was his own, and his own people did not accept him" (John 1:11). How many of us have really accepted him? According to the Pew Research Center's forum on *Religion & Public Life*, those who are religiously nonaffiliated, the "nones" (who say that their religious tradition is "nothing in particular") now constitute 23 percent of adult Americans and 35 percent of the Millennials, those born between 1981 and 1996. And the gap is growing. A study by the Pew Research Center in 2014 found that for every adult who is received into the Church, six Catholics leave. Another Pew study shows that less than half of Catholics are certain that one can have a personal relationship with God, and 58 percent of Catholics believe that only about 20 percent of their coreligionists have had a personal, life-changing encounter with Christ. If true, how sad this is.

GRACED MOMENTS

Each of us should ask ourselves if we have had such an encounter. Where have we been touched by grace? How has our life been changed? The incarnation means that God has entered space and time and human history; God is not distant, but nearer to us than we are to ourselves. We encounter him in those we meet every day. We have many epiphanies, that is, graced moments in our daily lives.

What is a graced moment? These are moments when we can recognize that Jesus Emmanuel, God, is with us. Grace is a way of describing the Holy Spirit. The Spirit reveals God to us, brings us to recognize and rejoice in the Divine Presence, and gives us a share in the divine life. The Spirit enlivens us, moves us to praise, worship, or service in some particular way; it expands our horizons to see more deeply and moves us to pray. These are signs of the Spirit's presence. But the Spirit is free; like the wind, it blows where it will (cf. John 3:8). Its presence is always a gift. Thus a graced moment is a moment in time or memory when we become aware that God's grace or Spirit has touched us; we become transparent through some experience. We stand in awe before a beauty that speaks of the Creator, or experience a gift that fills our hearts with gratitude, or gain an insight into God's love experienced in the love of a friend.

Some years ago, I was in New York City with some time to kill. Being an amateur historian with a special interest in the Second World War, I decided to go downtown and tour the U.S.S. Intrepid, a World War II Essex class carrier. Commissioned in 1943, the Intrepid survived five Kamikaze attacks and one torpedo strike, served in the Cold War and Vietnam, before finally being decommissioned in 1974. Today, it is the centerpiece of the Intrepid Sea, Air & Space Museum, docked at Pier 86 on the Hudson River.

I had a great time exploring the carrier's compartments, the exhibits in its hanger deck, and the planes on its flight deck. When I finally left the pier to head for the subway, I encountered a group protesting with chants and placards. One said, "The Intrepid Museum is a Monument to Death." With my liberal tendencies causing me some embarrassment, I decided to quietly slip away, minding my own business. But then, I thought, who, besides members of Dorothy Day's Catholic Worker movement, would be protesting such an exhibit? I was friends with the group in Los Angeles. So I looked up to check out the crowd, when suddenly someone yelled, "Father Rausch," and came rushing forward to give me a big hug. It was a young woman, a girl, really, whom I had taught at my university in Los Angeles some years before and hadn't seen since. She was now living with the Catholic Worker community in New York.

Our reunion was a graced moment, a reminder that beyond ideologies and politics and social commitments, friendship is deeper, that our lives have touched each other's and are intertwined, that a passing acquaintance can leave a lasting impression, that God's gracious presence so often transforms the ordinary to make it luminous and transparent.

Another story comes from another friend, now a theologian herself. A book she and a friend wrote on young women and Catholicism tells the story of a woman up at four o'clock in the morning nursing her restless infant son. Despite the early hour and her state, between sleep and consciousness, she found that she had been repeating over and over, "Take this and eat. This is my body." As her child clung to her, she said, "'So that's what that means'. ... After thirty-one years as a cradle Catholic, the Eucharist finally made sense."[2]

One way to appreciate these moments is the daily examination of conscience, or as it is often called today, a "Consciousness Examen," the one exercise that St. Ignatius told the members of his company that they should never omit. A Consciousness Examen is not a negative cataloguing of faults and sins, though we fall short every day, but a moment to ask, where has God been present in my life today, or have I experienced today any epiphanies? More than an examination of conscience, with its narrow moralistic sense, it is an exercise in discernment, an opening of the eyes of our spirit to recognize God's presence in our actions and affectivity, to see where God has been present in our day.

Such an examination of consciousness is a way of deepening our own spiritual identity by asking ourselves the following questions: How have I lived out my discipleship today? Where have I entered into Christ's paschal mystery in some moment of dying to self or rising to life? How might God be calling me into a more personal relationship? When did I experience love, goodness, truth, beauty, compassion, or communion with the transcendent? These are God's footprints, so to speak, like tracks in a cloud chamber, making the invisible perceptible. We experience God's presence often in a conversation with someone we have met, or in the quiet presence of a friend, or sometimes just resting quietly in God's presence.

Sometimes it is in an unexpected grace, or through a connection made with another, or in the quiet presence of a friend, or in a moment when I reached out to touch or heal another or simply be present. Where did I stand in awe before a beauty that speaks of the Creator or experience something that filled my heart with gratitude? Where did I gain an insight into God's love through the love of another? All these are epiphanies, graced moments.

Often this exercise, especially when performed at the end of the day, becomes a time of prayer. We find ourselves moved to praise and thanksgiving. Fr. Dennis Hamm, a Jesuit scripture professor at Creighton University, calls the Daily Examen a "rummaging for God." He likens it to "going through a drawer full of stuff, feeling around, looking for something that you are sure must be there."[3] There are various ways of making the Consciousness Examen. In the *Spiritual Exercises*, St. Ignatius suggests five points (no. 43).

THE CONSCIOUSNESS EXAMEN

My own preference is to make the Examen in the quiet of the night and keep it very simple. Make a break with your ordinary routines. Maybe go outside into the cool of the evening. First, ask God for enlightenment, that you might see. Second, review the day. What moments stand out? What experiences were especially memorable or significant? Where were you touched or moved? What awakened your love? What do you regret or what could you have done better? Finally, spend some time in thanksgiving, thanking God for his presence in special moments and encounters with others, and ask for the grace to make amends where you might have fallen short. Often, what we experience from such a review of the day is not guilt but gratitude.

The incarnation means that the transcendent God has entered into creation and transformed it. Thus, God is not distant. Jesus the Word has pitched his tent among us and meets us in word, symbol, and sacrament. Even more, this Jesus has gathered us into his Body and identifies with the poor, the outcast, and the persecuted. We encounter him in our brothers and sisters. In a poem titled "The Vast Ocean Begins Just Outside Our Church: The Eucharist," Mary Oliver says in part,

Incarnation

I want
to see Jesus,
maybe in the clouds

Or on the shore,
just walking,
beautiful man

And clearly
someone else
besides.

On hard days
I ask myself
if I ever will.

Also there are times
my body whispers to me
that I have.

8

THE MOTHER OF JESUS

Years ago, I spent a sabbatical year at the World Council of Churches' Ecumenical Institute at Bossey, Switzerland. A program called simply the "Graduate School" brought together for five months young church leaders from around the world—parish workers, catechists, teachers, ordained and lay ministers, and so on. I remember especially a Eucharist celebrated by an Australian Methodist liturgist, one of the visiting faculty members, at which a beautiful young woman by the name of Maria, a Reformed pastor from Indonesia, read a passage from the Book of Revelation (12:1–17) that in the Catholic tradition has often been seen as referring to Mary. The picture of the woman adorned with the sun, the moon under her feet, and a crown of stars on her head, often represented in Catholic art, is generally understood today as referring to Israel who would give birth to the Messiah, and thus to God's people under attack from Satan. But I was moved to see a Protestant woman, bearing Mary's name, reading from this passage. While one doesn't usually find devotion to Mary among Protestants, this graced moment seemed an exception.

MARY IN SCRIPTURE AND TRADITION

Mary, the mother of Jesus, has long fascinated Christians. Scripture tells us very little about her, although the author of John's Gospel, who never refers to her by name, shows Jesus entrusting the Beloved Disciple to her from the cross (John 19:27), something that has found great resonance in the Christian tradition. As early as the second century, one finds Christian imagination focused on Mary's role in the story of Jesus. The apocryphal Gospel of James tells stories of her birth, the presentation in the temple, and the names of her parents, Joachim and Anna, and explains the "brothers and sisters of Jesus" as children of Joseph by a previous marriage. This work must have been very popular, as today more than one hundred fifty Greek manuscripts are extent. Other apocryphal works from the second and third centuries attempt to fill in details from her life and what they describe as Jesus's miraculous birth. Stories of Mary's death, or "dormition," and assumption into heaven date from the fourth century.

The fathers of the Church often reflected on the image of Mary, though always from a christological perspective. Ignatius of Antioch (d. 110) emphasized that Mary truly carried Jesus in her womb and truly gave him birth, to counter the Docetist teaching that he was not truly human. Just as Paul developed a parallelism between Adam and Jesus, Justin Martyr (d. 165) and Irenaeus of Lyons (d. 202) played on the parallelism between the virgin Eve and the Virgin Mary. Irenaeus, Tertullian (d. 225), Hippolytus (d. 235), and Augustine (d. 430) all associated her with the Church.

There is evidence of Christians asking Mary's intercession as early as the early third century. A Greek text from this time has a beautiful prayer, the *Sub Tuum Praesidium*, used by both the Eastern and Western churches, addressing her as Mother of God (*theotokos*):

We fly to thy patronage,
O holy Mother of God;
despise not our petitions
in our necessities,
but deliver us always from dangers,
O glorious and blessed Virgin,
Amen.

This prayer is echoed in the medieval *Memorare*: "Remember O most gracious Virgin Mary, that never was it known that anyone who fled to your protections..." By the fourth century, a cult of Mary, expressed in both art and prayer, was developing, especially in the East, while the Middle Ages saw a popular cult of the Virgin as intercessor emerging in the West, one that stressed also her role in Christ's work of salvation.

The Reformers sought to safeguard the unique role of Christ in redemption, with the result that devotion to Mary in the Reformation traditions virtually disappeared. Still, Luther kept an image of Mary on the wall of his study and frequently wrote about her, and there is evidence today of a new interest in Mary among some Evangelicals.[1]

CATHOLIC MARIOLOGY

If Marian devotion in Catholicism has sometimes become over sentimentalized or theologically problematic, threatening to displace the central role of Jesus, it still remains an important part of the tradition. Imagine a Catholic church without a statue of Mary. Consider the many expressions of Marian piety that would be lost: the rosary; processions; feasts in the liturgy; icons of the Madonna and child; hymns; chapels, churches, and universities dedicated to her name; official Marian doctrines (perpetual virginity, Mother of God, immaculate conception, and the assumption); and various apparitions that the Church has made her own. What is it about the image of the mother of Jesus that it has so deeply stamped the Catholic tradition?

First, Mary is revered because of her closeness to Jesus. She, who bore him in her womb, brought him into the world, raised him, taught him to value his tradition, and loved him into adulthood, enjoyed a special relationship with the Word become flesh. The stories in the apocryphal Gospels reflect the fascination of the early Christians with Mary's role in the story of Jesus. By venerating the importance of that irreplaceable maternal bond, the Church highlights its importance in all of our lives. Relationships are real; they form and shape us. The Church's insistence on the importance of family life underlines the importance of these relationships. So also we help to form and shape each other, for better or worse.

The life at Nazareth remains hidden, but we can enter into it imaginatively, contemplating scenes from the life of the holy family. We can imagine Mary cradling her child, helping him take his first steps, dealing with the disappointments and hurts of childhood, and teaching him to pray. Joseph also played an important role in his life. Consider how important a father is in the life of a boy. Joseph shared his trade with the young Jesus, teaching him to use his tools, giving him a love for good wood and craftsmanship, modeling integrity in his personal life. From him he learned what it meant to be a man, strong but gentle, tender even. We can imagine this family about their daily tasks: at meals, sharing the blessings of daily life, a cool evening, a beautiful sunset, each other's company. In contemplating these deeply human events in the lives of Jesus, Mary, and Joseph, we connect with similar events in our own. And Mary, who shares fully in her Son's risen life, is still close to him.

Second, Mary's very closeness to Jesus makes her a powerful intercessor. We can call on her as the Church has done from its earliest years for her help and prayers. The oldest prayer to Mary, the *Sub Tuum Praesidium*, dates from the third century as we have seen. The *Salve Regina* or Hail Holy Queen may date back to the eleventh century. It was chanted in monastic communities at the close of Compline, or sometimes by the monks as they made their way back to their dormitory or cells after Compline. Cistercians still sing it at the end of the day in a darkened church, and the prayer is said at the end of the Rosary. The *Memorare*, derived from a longer fifteenth-century prayer, was popularized by Claude Bernard, a French priest educated by the Jesuits who ministered to prisoners, especially those facing capital punishment. Most popular is the *Ave Maria* or Hail Mary, whose origins are obscure. The first verses are from Scripture; they include the Archangel Gabriel's greeting to Mary at the annunciation and Elizabeth's greeting at the visitation, both in Luke's Gospel. The remaining verses, "Holy Mary, Mother of God, pray for us sinners now and at the hour of our death," were added later. The prayer first appears in print in 1495 in Savonarola's *Esposizione sopra l'Ave Maria*. The prayer appears in a different form in the Orthodox and Eastern Catholic traditions.

A final reason for her popularity may be, as Andrew Greeley once suggested, that the cult of Mary gives expression to the feminine dimension of the divine, too often unnoticed.[2] This is not to suggest that God is feminine. But given the patriarchal nature of the Church's theological language, with its gendered language of the Trinity, devotion to Mary offers believers a sense for the feminine qualities of the divine. It suggests the maternal nature of God, even a tender, nurturing dimension not usually expressed in our God language.

There is a certain elastic, malleable quality to the image of Mary in the Catholic tradition. Raymond Brown once traced the "symbolic trajectory" of her image as it was adapted to concretize the ideals of Christian discipleship in different ages in the life of the Church. For the ascetics of the desert in the early Church, she took on the characteristics of an Egyptian nun. In the chivalrous culture of the Middle Ages, she became "Our Lady" to the knights, a symbol of chaste love. In the twentieth century, she has been honored as a model of family life. More recently, she has been portrayed as an example of the liberated woman in a letter of the American bishops.[3]

The image of Our Lady of Guadalupe, so popular with Mexicans and Mexican Americans, gave the religion of the *conquistadores* an indigenous expression by clothing the mother of Jesus in the dress and symbols of the indigenous people of Mexico. Some regard her as the Woman of the Apocalypse, "clothed with the sun, with the moon under her feet, and on her head a crown of twelve stars" (Rev 12:1). But, to the Mexican people, this Mary is a brown-skinned *mestiza*, *La Morenita*, "the little brown one." She is dressed simply, a maternity band around her waist as a sign of the child to come. She stands on the moon and blocks the light of the sun (both deities worshipped by the indigenous peoples), a sign of her superiority to the old religion, and thus the superiority of Christianity. So also the stars on her mantle are a sign of the beginning of a new era. The origin of the image, whether it was painted or miraculously produced, is controverted. However, it does not really matter; the image has long served to give an indigenous expression to the European religion of Mexico's conquerors, making it their own.

Behind these layers of the Marian tradition we find the story of Miriam, the young Jewish girl—perhaps about fourteen or fifteen— who gave birth to Jesus. We know almost nothing about her experience. Luke's story of the annunciation, with the Archangel Gabriel telling the Virgin that she was to be the mother of the Son of God, is one of the most frequently represented subjects of Christian art. But just what Mary experienced remains hidden from us. Was she visited by an angelic messenger? Was her pregnancy a mystery even to her? Certainly others saw her as an unmarried girl, as the story of Joseph's dilemma in Matthew's Gospel suggests (Matt 1:18–25).

Luke gives us an insight into Mary's interior life, telling us that she continued to reflect on events in her life that must have remained mysterious. At the end of the story of the nativity and the visit of the shepherds, he tells us that "Mary treasured all these words and pondered them in her heart" (Luke 2:19), and again, after the finding of the boy Jesus in the temple, he says something similar (Luke 2:51). Whatever her actual experience, her openness to God's presence in her life and maternal care for the child she bore forever ennobled and transformed our humanity. She remains a model for us all.

Here are selected verses from two Marian poems: one very traditional, the other by Gerard Manley Hopkins:

JESUS

Lovely Lady dressed in blue—
Teach me how to pray!
God was just your little boy,
And you know the way.

—Mary Dixon Thayer, "Lovely Lady Dressed in Blue"[4]

A mother came to mould
Those limbs like ours which are
What must make our daystar
Much dearer to mankind;
Whose glory bare would blind
Or less would win man's mind.
Through her we may see him
Made sweeter, not made dim,
And her hand leaves his light
Sifted to suit our sight.

—Gerard Manley Hopkins, "The Blessed Virgin
Compared to the Air We Breathe"

9

THE BEATITUDES

The Beatitudes are at the very heart of the good news Jesus preached. With a common source in the "Q" tradition, they come in two versions. Luke's version is briefer, simpler; it may be closer to the words of Jesus, with its emphasis on "the poor," "the hungry," and "those who weep." Matthew has expanded the tradition with material from the Psalms. Both versions are rooted in God's special concern for the poor so evident in the Old Testament.

Without losing their original focus, the Beatitudes model what should be a way of life for the disciples. For Pope Benedict, they also have a profoundly christological character, as they describe how Jesus lived.[1] Finally, it is important that we don't regard the Beatitudes as merely historical; they are equally pertinent today, with so many who are disadvantaged, discriminated against, or persecuted. The poor have not been forgotten by God, who always hears their cry. We will focus here on the Beatitudes as presented by Matthew (5:3–12):

> Blessed are the poor in spirit, for theirs is the kingdom of heaven.
>
> Blessed are those who mourn, for they will be comforted.
>
> Blessed are the meek, for they will inherit the earth.

Blessed are those who hunger and thirst for righteousness, for they will be filled.

Blessed are the merciful, for they will receive mercy.

Blessed are the pure in heart, for they will see God.

Blessed are the peacemakers, for they will be called children of God.

Blessed are those who are persecuted for righteousness' sake, for theirs is the kingdom of heaven.

Blessed are you when people revile you and persecute you and utter all kinds of evil against you falsely on my account. Rejoice and be glad, for your reward is great in heaven, for in the same way they persecuted the prophets who were before you.

GOD'S CONCERN FOR JUSTICE

Woven through the Beatitudes is God's concern for justice, a regular theme throughout the Old Testament. Both the law and the prophets stress God's care for the vulnerable—the widow, the orphan, and the alien or stranger in the land. Without husband, parents, or people, they were alone and powerless in a tribal society. God reminds the Israelites that they themselves were once aliens, immigrants really, in the land of Egypt, and promises to hear the cry of the needy and oppressed.

The law is full of concern for the disadvantaged. An Israelite is not to demand interest, like an extortioner, from a poor neighbor on a loan. They are not to violate the rights of the alien or orphan, nor take the clothing of a widow as a pledge (Deut 24:17). If you take your poor neighbor's cloak as security for a loan, you shall return it before the sun goes down, for it may be the poor neighbor's only clothing to use as cover (Exod 22:26–27). The Israelites are commanded not to second-pick their wheat or vines, but leave something for the poor and the alien (Lev 19:10; Deut 24:19–21). Every seventh year is to be a sabbatical year in which Hebrew slaves are freed and the fields left fallow and unharvested to benefit the poor (Exod 23:10; Deut 15:1–18). According to Isaiah, their very worship is loathsome when they come before God with bloody hands and ignore the plea of the fatherless and the widow (Isa 1:11–23; cf. Amos 5:21–25).

The psalms celebrate a God who never forgets the needy (Ps 10:17), who rescues the poor from the strong (35:10), and delivers those who have no one to help them (72:12), securing for them justice (140:12), giving them food, setting prisoners free, lifting those who are bowed down, and watching over the immigrant, the orphan, and the widow (146:7–9). These themes are echoed in the preaching of Jesus, in the Beatitudes and in his great discourse on the judgment of the nations, when he says we will be judged on whether or not we fed the hungry, gave drink to the thirsty, welcomed the stranger, clothed the naked, and visited those in prison (Matt 25:31–46). Let's look more closely at each of the Beatitudes.

Blessed Are the Poor in Spirit, for Theirs Is the Kingdom of Heaven

Matthew's addition of "in spirit" to the words about the poor should not be read as a spiritualizing of the Beatitudes. With his profound sense of Jesus's fulfillment of the Old Testament, Matthew is mindful of the *anawim* or poor of the Old Testament, those without any earthly power: the humble, marginalized, or vulnerable who are completely dependent on God. They come before God with empty hands, adding a religious dimension to their poverty. In his apostolic exhortation *Evangelii gaudium*, Pope Francis says that the kingdom of God is about loving the God who reigns in our world; to the extent that he reigns within us, "the life of society will be a setting for universal fraternity, justice, peace and dignity." The mission of Jesus is to inaugurate the kingdom; ours is to proclaim the good news that the kingdom is at hand (no. 180). The pope wants a Church "which is poor and for the poor. They have much to teach us" (no. 198).

Thus God's promise doesn't exclude the millions who live today *in extremis*—those who lack food, shelter, basic sanitation, just wages, medical care, and education for their children (in a word, a *future*)—nor those who live in slavery today, more than at any time in human history. These include women and children who are trafficked for the pleasure and profit of others, and people who are trapped in bonded labor from which they can never escape, with even their children required to work long hours. Jesus says theirs is the kingdom of heaven.

Blessed Are Those Who Mourn, for They Will Be Comforted

Closely related to the poor are those who mourn. This includes those who refuse to give in to evil, who suffer injustice, violence, and oppression; they can only await God's intervention on their behalf for an end to their suffering. The apparent triumph of evil is painful to them; in the Old Testament, they long for God's promised salvation, to be revealed in the messianic age of salvation. Today, they might also include those dealing with personal tragedy; others are the victims of poverty, injustice, and violence, as well as those who suffer discrimination or even face death for their faith. They will be comforted.

Blessed Are the Meek, for They Will Inherit the Earth

Those who are meant by the "meek" may not be immediately clear. The English word suggests those who are shy, timid, or nonassertive. But the Greek, *praus*, has the sense of being humble, slow to anger, or those whose social status limits their ability to defend their rights. Their very vulnerability and social situation limits what they are able to do. In this sense, the meek are closely related to the poor in spirit and those who mourn. Indeed, *praus* is used in the Septuagint, the Greek translation of the Hebrew Scriptures, to translate *anawim* in the Hebrew.

But there is also strength here, as in the figure of Jesus, who said, "I am meek and humble of heart" (Matt 11:29, NABRE), Jesus who emptied himself, taking the form of a slave, becoming obedient even unto death on a cross (Phil 2:6–11). Jesus was not timid, but renounced all violence, including the violence used against him, asking his Father to forgive those who persecuted him.

Blessed Are Those Who Hunger and Thirst for Righteousness, for They Will Be Filled

For Matthew, righteousness means to live in accordance with God's will. Those who try to do so, often suffer at the hands of the wicked and the powerful. Like Jesus, they are victims of injustice. In contemporary terms, they would include the millions who suffered from persecution, violence, and death from the Armenian genocide as the century opened, the 2 to 7 million who died of hunger in Ukraine under Stalin, the 6 million victims of Hitler's vicious persecution of the Jews of Europe in the Holocaust or Shoah, to more recent victims in Cambodia, the former Yugoslavia, Rwanda, and the Sudan.

The fathers of the Church saw Jesus in solidarity with all those who have suffered throughout history, and his victory over sin and death is ultimately theirs. Theologians such as Johann Baptist Metz, Jon Sobrino, Elizabeth Johnson, Peter Phan, and Terrance Tilley stress the social dimensions of the kingdom of God already breaking into the world through the ministry of Jesus. Among those who hunger and thirst for justice or righteousness today, we could include the hundreds of thousands of immigrants, the many who still suffer from racial prejudice, as well as gays and lesbians who continue to experience discrimination, sometimes even in their families, and women who in so many countries today are still second-class citizens or victims of violence, even rape.

In his encyclical on hope, *Spe salvi*, Pope Benedict XVI describes how the triumph of the scientific method as well as the rationalism of the French Revolution and the Enlightenment secularized Christian hope in God's salvation, substituting a hope in salvation through human progress. He insists that the injustices of history will not have the final word.

He links God's justice to the resurrection of Jesus in whom "God now reveals his true face in the figure of the sufferer who shares man's God-forsaken condition by taking it upon himself. This innocent sufferer has attained the certitude of hope: there is a God, and God can create justice in a way that we cannot conceive, yet we can begin to grasp it through faith." Indeed, Benedict says, "I'm convinced that the question of justice constitutes the essential argument, in any case, the strongest argument, in favor of faith in eternal life" (no. 43). He quotes, as we noted earlier, Dostoevsky's remark in *The Brothers Karamazov* that "evildoers, in the end, do not sit at table at the eternal banquet beside their victims without distinction, as though nothing had happened" (no. 44).

Too often, conservative American Christianity has reduced the Christian idea of salvation to an individualistic "being saved" and going to heaven. Others preach the "Prosperity Gospel." How different is the rich eschatological hope of the Christian Scriptures. Yes, the idea of the resurrection of the dead is central; we hope to share in the resurrection of the body of which Christ Jesus is the "first fruits" (1 Cor 15:20–22). But the fullness of God's salvation means also the victory of justice, that marvelous day in God's future when God will dwell with the human race and wipe away every tear from their eyes and "death will be no more; / mourning and crying and pain will be no more, / for the first things have passed away" (Rev 21:4).

Blessed Are the Merciful, for They Will Receive Mercy

In his opening address of the Second Vatican Council, Pope John XXIII said that the Church "prefers to make use of the medicine of mercy rather than that of severity."[2] For Pope Francis, mercy is at the heart of the divine. To help others experience this, in 2015 he summoned the Church into a "Year of Mercy."

The theme of God's mercy is a constant in both the Old and the New Testaments. It is another word for God's loving kindness and abiding love, as in the psalms: "The LORD is merciful and gracious, / slow to anger and abounding in steadfast love" (Ps 103:8). It describes the very nature of God who reaches out to creatures to show his love. In Walter Kasper's words, "God's mercy is the power of God that sustains, protects, promotes, builds up, and creates life anew. It bursts the logic of human justice, which entails the punishment and death of the sinner."[3]

Because Jesus is one with God, "consubstantial with the Father," he becomes the mirror of God's mercy. Matthew twice shows Jesus saying of the Father, "I desire mercy, not sacrifice" (Matt 9:13; 12:7). He showed God's mercy in his earthly ministry, assuring the poor and the hungry of God's special love, healing the sick, freeing those burdened by oppressive spirits, bringing back to society those estranged by disease or rigid religious rules, restoring to the widow her dead son. Typical is his reaction to the woman taken in adultery, disregarding the penalty of the law, embarrassing those who condemned her, and letting her go (John 8:2–11).

To speak of God's mercy is to speak of God's love, God's selfless, dynamic love that offers us a share in the divine life. The doctrine of the Trinity points to this love as the inner life of God. Relationality is at the heart of the mystery of the divine.

Thus, Francis's call for a Year of Mercy should touch each of us personally. Mercy takes us out of ourselves. It means breaking out of our self-preoccupations, reaching out compassionately to others, being willing to forgive, to reconcile, to make right, and to heal. But it is also a call for the Church itself to present a more merciful face to the world. This was one of this pope's goals for the two Synods of Bishops on the family, the Extraordinary Synod in 2014 and the General Synod a year later. The Church also needs to learn to show a more merciful face to those who are "different" or powerless—gays and lesbians, women, those who have suffered from sexual abuse at the hands of clergy, immigrants and the undocumented, especially those the Church itself has marginalized.

Blessed Are the Pure in Heart, for They Will See God

As opposed to a mere ritual purity, being clean of heart suggests purity of intention, a simple desire to do what is right, and a faithfulness to God's will. Those whose hearts are pure will see God, that is, they will come into that personal relationship with God who remains always mystery. Thus, knowing God is more than a question of pure rationality or the knowledge that comes from ordinary experience. God's will cannot be reduced to rules and traditions. Jesus taught that a person is defiled not by violations of the law such as unwashed hands, but by evil thoughts, murder, adultery, unchastity, theft, false witness, blasphemy, all of which come from the heart (Matt 15:10–20). And how do we know what is God's will? For Thomas Merton, "whatever is demanded by truth, by justice, by mercy, or by love must surely be taken to be willed by God. To consent to His will is, then, to consent to be true, or to speak truth, or at least to seek it."[4]

Strongly influenced by Plato and Augustine, Joseph Ratzinger has long stressed the role of the will in knowing. In his *Jesus of Nazareth*, he argues that the human person is a unity of soul and body, matter and spirit. The body needs the discipline of the spirit; God's mystery is disclosed to those who love the good and seek the truth, those who seek to follow the person's fundamental orientation to the true, the good, and the beautiful. He cites this beatitude, commenting that "the organ for seeing God is the heart. The intellect alone is not enough."[5] How often do we see this born out in those whose lives are uncomplicated, the poor who often astound us with their generosity, those of simple, trusting faith, whose lives reflect a basic goodness?

Blessed Are the Peacemakers, for They Will Be Called Children of God

In the Penitential Rite of the liturgy, we invoke Christ who "came to reconcile us to the Father and to one and other." Christ is the Prince of Peace, the one who overcame sin, which estranges people from one another and is responsible for so much violence. As his disciples, we are also called to be peacemakers in our families, our communities, and our world. St. Paul tells us that just as God has reconciled us to himself through Christ, so he has given us a ministry of reconciliation, entrusting us with the message of reconciliation (2 Cor 5:18–19).

Peacemakers have the ability to change the hearts of another, to gentle and open them. We greatly need peacemakers today. We think of the scourge of terrorism that leaves so many victims in its wake, men and women in suicide vests and bomb-laden automobiles whose hatreds, based on ideologies or misinterpreted religious traditions, take such a bloody toll of the innocent; or that of the wars that seem to go on without end; or the political rancor that fractures our political processes, leaving government ineffective; or the racism that still causes tensions and even violence in our society.

The last two beatitudes speak again of those persecuted for the sake of righteousness, or for their discipleship, echoing what we have already seen. Again, in proclaiming God's care for the poor, for those who bear injustice and persecution, who seek peace and reconciliation, the Beatitudes give us the ethics of the kingdom. They call us to solidarity with one another, to a new sense of community that goes beyond religion or race or culture or sexual orientation to recognize ourselves as children of a loving Father. We know that there will never be perfect justice in this life. Our hope in God's justice is an eschatological hope.

At an audience with a group of Catholics and Lutherans from Germany, Pope Francis said, "'It's hypocrisy to call yourself a Christian and chase away a refugee or someone seeking help.' He went on, 'You cannot be a Christian without practicing the Beatitudes. You cannot be a Christian without doing what Jesus teaches us in Matthew 25,' which is to feed the hungry, clothe the naked and welcome the stranger."[6]

A SPIRITUALITY OF THE BEATITUDES

The Beatitudes speak of God's mercy breaking in, a mercy that is already transformative. This is the great lesson of L'Arche. Now a global movement in which young men and women "assistants" live in community with others who are handicapped, L'Arche was founded by

Jean Vanier at Trosly-Breuil in France in 1964. Vanier has long claimed that the Beatitudes are at the heart of Jesus's message, and at the heart of L'Arche. The assistants, those men and women, most of them quite young, who make a covenant to stay at L'Arche for a certain length of time, are a marvelous group. Many of them live in foyers or households with the handicapped, not so much to take care of them but to live in community with them. They are more than helpers or social workers. They dress simply in cords and blue jeans, sandals, and, for some of the women, long cotton dresses. They get only a little spending money, have one day off a week, and one weekend off a month. To see them at table with the handicapped or bringing those to church who want to go is to experience a very deep goodness.

Entering into community with others who are handicapped is healing for the assistants as well as for the handicapped themselves. They discover that the handicapped are often living the Beatitudes more closely than those who are "well." Many of these vulnerable people are incapable of rational understanding or complex thinking. Some show warmth and affection from the time you meet them, smiling shyly, holding your hand. Others are more reserved, can't speak properly, or can't communicate their feelings. But they are keenly perceptive, are aware of your presence, and seem at times to have a kind of telepathy for the feelings of another. When they find that they are loved and cared for, they communicate in the language of the heart.[7] When they do, both assistants and the handicapped come to experience God's presence.

Always a realist, Vanier recognizes that the handicapped can often be difficult. But their vulnerability helps the assistants to discover their own. As Vanier has written, "When the handicapped person calls forth our darkness, anger and/or anguish, we discover the truth about ourselves."[8] For it is precisely in our brokenness, rejection, and abandonment that we can discover the love of God who, in Jesus, entered so deeply into our humanity, Jesus, who calls happy those who mourn, are persecuted for justice, or are clean of heart. This is the spirituality of the Beatitudes.

10

Resurrection

Some years ago, I accompanied a group of students to El Salvador on an "alternative spring break," designed to give our students a grassroots experience of how people in developing countries live today. During our week there, the students learned firsthand the story of Msgr. Oscar Romero, San Salvador's martyred archbishop. Romero was an unlikely saint. Very traditional in his early years as a priest, he was recommended by the government for the position of archbishop, figuring that he would be easily controlled. But as an auxiliary bishop and later archbishop, he became more aware of the suffering of the poor of El Salvador. He underwent a conversion after his good friend, Jesuit Father Rutilio Grande, was assassinated on March 12, 1977, driving back after Mass from the little town of Aguilares. Accompanying him in the jeep was an elderly man and a fifteen-year-old boy, both killed, and three children to whom they had given a ride. Grande was hit by twelve bullets.

AN UNLIKELY SAINT

Grande's death changed Romero. He went to the church in El Paisnal, where the three bodies were laid out, and spent hours listening to the people. Afterward, he cancelled all Masses in the archdiocese for the following Sunday, in place of a single memorial Mass for the three victims, to be celebrated in the cathedral. He demanded that the government investigate the murders, though it never did. But this once conservative professor, now the archbishop, began to imitate Grande's ministry; he listened to his people, walked in their shoes, and shared their sorrows. In his sermons, frequently using the archdiocesan radio station, he spoke out powerfully on behalf of his people, especially the poor. Before long he too was receiving death threats. On March 24, 1980, a lone gunman assassinated him while he was celebrating Mass at the Hospital of Divine Providence in San Salvador.

Over his grave in the crypt of the Cathedral of San Salvador is the legend in red marble, "*Sentir con la Iglesia,*" usually translated as "think with the church." The phrase is Ignatian. Though not in the original text of the *Spiritual Exercises*, it was added as a subtitle to introduce Ignatius's "rules for thinking with the church," and would have been familiar to Romero who had frequently made the *Exercises*. While most English speakers understand the phrase to mean giving assent to official church teaching, for Romero the Spanish verb *sentir* would have suggested a deeper meaning. *Sentir* means to experience, to feel. In context, it should be translated "to feel with the church," and for Romero, "church" meant the suffering people of God for whom he was bishop. The Church was not the hierarchy, the other bishops, Rome; it was the people with whom he was united. Romero experienced the grace of the resurrection in his ministry as bishop. Knowing that his life was in danger, he said, "If they kill me, I will rise in the people." And he did. Today, his picture is everywhere in San Salvador. Pope Francis beatified him as a martyr on May 23, 2015.

RESURRECTION OF THE BODY

In John's Gospel, the story of Jesus raising Lazarus is a symbol of the final resurrection when we are raised up in our bodies to be with

God. This is our most profound Christian hope. But today, few believe in the resurrection of the body. Many believe that it is some vague spirit that lives on; others believe in angels, but not in God, which makes no sense. But Christian faith begins with the resurrection of Jesus; without it, we would know nothing about him. Paul calls him the "first fruits" of the resurrection from the dead (1 Cor 15:20–23). We confess in the creed, that fundamental expression of our faith, "I believe in the resurrection of the body and life everlasting." We can't imagine it, but we can understand it. In John's Gospel, the risen Jesus still bears his wounds in his body. He can relate to our own wounds, our pain, what we have endured or suffered.

But the resurrection as a symbol means much more. Glorified at the Father's right hand, Jesus is still one of us. Our destiny is to be with God—in our bodies, with our memories, our relationships, most of all, our relationship with our loving God, which is what heaven means. The story of Jesus raising his friend Lazarus is not just the miracle of bringing his friend back to life. It is a story of transforming grace, the grace that sets us free, that breaks the bonds of sin and death. It is God's Spirit that gives us a share in God's life. Pope Leo the Great said that the "foreshadowing of the future resurrection should appear in the church. What is to happen to our bodies should now take place in our hearts."[1] It did for Oscar Romero, turning the conservative professor into the fearless pastor and martyr. And we heard other stories like his in El Salvador.

VISITING "THE UCA"

We visited the Jesuit University of Central America, "the UCA," a beautiful tree-shaded campus where one night in 1989, soldiers of the U.S.-trained and equipped Atlacatl Battalion invaded the campus, dragged six Jesuits from their beds, and shot them in the garden behind their residence, later killing their cook and her sixteen-year-old daughter, who were spending the night in an adjacent parlor for safety. As we prayed quietly in the rose garden, planted by the husband of the murdered Elba Ramos, one of our students broke down in silent tears. Afterward, we celebrated Eucharist in the Chapel of the Martyrs, a short distance from the residence and the garden where they died. It was another graced moment.

Besides our quiet liturgy, two experiences from this trip will long remain with me. One was our visit to two student communities, the Casa de La Solidaridad and Romero House. The inspiration for both came from Dean Brackley, one of five North American Jesuits who came as volunteers to the UCA some months after the murder of Fr. Ignacio Ellacuría and his companions, to continue their work. The Casa is a program for students from Jesuit schools in the United States who come for a semester. In addition to the emphasis on academics, spirituality, and community, they spend two days a week at "praxis sites," giving them the opportunity to become directly involved with the poor. Graduates of the program are working today in various parts of the world. One was hired by the president of an African country, interested in her research paper on the special needs of African women. Another was in charge of Jesuit Refugee Services in Jordan. Two are now Jesuits.

The other program, Romero House, brings together Salvadoran students from the campo or country with scholarships; these are young men and women who otherwise would have no opportunity for higher education. They live in community for five years, spending two months living with the American students next door at the Casa. Brackley, who died of cancer in 2011, said to the U.S. students at the Casa, "I hope this experience has broken your hearts. I hope it's allowed you to fall in love again. I hope it's ruined you for life."

These are resurrection experiences in which we see hope arising from tragedy, a promising future out of pain, life coming out of death. St. Paul talks of knowing Christ and the power of his resurrection, sharing in his sufferings by being conformed to his death, that we might attain the resurrection from the dead (cf. Phil 3:10–11). We experience that grace whenever we die to all those evils that separate us from God and each other, whether liquor, drugs, sex, self-absorption, the hookup culture, rebellion, the mindless pursuit of wealth, or a lack of responsibility for ourselves and for the world in which we live. As Thomas Merton wrote, "That I should be the contemporary of Auschwitz, Hiroshima, Viet Nam and the Watts riots, are things about which I was not first consulted. Yet they are also events in which, whether I like it or not, I am deeply and personally involved."[2] We might say the same thing today about the racism that is still present in our nation, about conflict between religions, about the growing gulf between the very rich and the poor.

Too often, we reduce sin to breaking rules. But that is to trivialize a far more serious reality. In Hebrew and Greek, *to sin* means "to miss the mark, to get lost, so that one does not arrive at one's destination," which, of course, is God. We think of sin as an exercise of our freedom, but it really means to lose our freedom, that spiritual freedom to respond to the Spirit of which St. Ignatius speaks in the *Spiritual Exercises*; it means to become trapped, captured, or bound. Sin is whatever alienates us from God and one another, and from ourselves. These are the deaths from which Christ sets us free. This is what he offers us now and in the world to come.

In our reflections during our week in El Salvador, the students remarked on the passionate faith of the people they had met, their warmth, their pride in their country, the ways they welcomed us. And they talked about their own struggles with faith. One said faith was like riding a bicycle up a hill; you only make progress or go back. Another, who after a long search was preparing for baptism at Easter, said that he realized at the cathedral that Catholicism was a world Church, celebrating the same Eucharist around the world; he felt like he was coming home. Summing up their experience, one student said, "We're just human. We belong to each other. We need to care for each other." This is to experience the Jesus who walks with us still. This is to experience the resurrection.

> May Christ who walks
> on wounded feet
> walk with you on the road.
> May the Christ who serves

with wounded hands
stretch out your hands to serve.
May the Christ who loves
with a wounded heart
open your hearts to love.
May you see the face of Christ
in everyone you meet,
and may everyone you meet
see the face of Christ in you.

—Traditional Celtic Prayer

11

PASCHAL MYSTERY

> Do you not know that all of us who have been baptized into
> Christ Jesus were baptized into his death? Therefore we have
> been buried with him by baptism into death, so that, just as
> Christ was raised from the dead by the glory of the Father, so we
> too might walk in newness of life.
>
> —Romans 6:3–4

The paschal mystery refers to Jesus's passage from his life lived in union with the Father, through death, to his risen life at the Father's right hand. Recent focus on the historical Jesus in theology, with its emphasis on the humanity of Jesus, has deepened our appreciation of the paschal mystery. Thus, it also refers to the mystery of our own passage through death to life.

BAPTIZED INTO THE DEATH OF JESUS

In the Catholic funeral liturgy, the priest or deacon meets the family and coffin of the deceased at the door of the church. He blesses the coffin with holy water, and then says, "In baptism, (name) was buried with Christ; may he (or she) also share in his resurrection." These few words recall the paschal mystery that stands at the center of our Christian faith, our incorporation into the death and resurrection of Jesus.

The term *paschal* is rooted in the Hebrew *pesach* or "Passover"; thus the paschal mystery is a way of referring to Jesus's Passover to everlasting life. The New Testament has frequent references to Jesus as the new Passover. Paul says that Christ, our paschal lamb, has been sacrificed (1 Cor 5:7). John parallels his death, with his bones unbroken, to the preparation of the paschal lambs in the temple (John 19:31–33). The author of 1 Peter speaks of Christ as "a lamb without defect or blemish" (1 Pet 1:19).

Perhaps Paul expresses best the paschal mystery in the citation we began with, but it is a theme that runs through his letters. In Philippians, he speaks about giving up his own claims to righteousness based on observance of the law, to a new righteousness based on faith in Christ; he says that he desires "to know Christ and the power of his resurrection and the sharing of his sufferings by becoming like him in his death, if somehow I may attain the resurrection from the dead" (Phil 3:10–11; cf. Rom 8:17; Col 2:12).

What is this idea of passing through death to the life of the resurrection? First of all, death is something that each of us must ultimately face. Our mortality, much as we might like to ignore it, especially when swept away by the excitement of youth, is simply inescapable. Paul writes that death came into the world as a result of sin (Rom 5:12), but it is also intrinsic to our mortal existence. The German existentialist Martin Heidegger described our being-in-the-world or "*dasein*" as a being-toward death. Not even Jesus, God's only beloved son, could escape it, precisely because he shared our humanity, like us in all things but sin (cf. Heb 4:15).

This notion of life through death is also echoed in the Gospels. Jesus says repeatedly, if you want to be my disciple, you must deny yourself, take up your cross, and follow me (Mark 8:34; Matt 16:24). Luke, sensitive to the requirement of the life of discipleship, adds the word "daily" (Luke 9:23). To this saying, Jesus adds "those who want to save their life will lose it, and those who lose their life for my sake will save it"

(Luke 9:24). This involves a willingness to embrace the suffering symbolized by the cross. At the Last Supper, Jesus speaks of drinking again of the fruit of the vine "new in the kingdom of God" (Mark 14:25), thus on the other side of his approaching death.

John's Gospel has the same message, though in different words. On the eve of his passion, Jesus says to the disciples, "Very truly, I tell you, unless a grain of wheat falls into the earth and dies, it remains just a single grain; but if it dies, it bears much fruit" (John 12:24), adding "Whoever serves me must follow me, and where I am, there will my servant be also" (John 12:26). The language here echoes the rural imagery that runs through the Gospels.

DOES GOD NEED SACRIFICE?

At the heart of Christian faith is the idea that Jesus through his life, death, and resurrection saves us from sin and death, establishes a new covenant, and brings us salvation. But the sacrificial language the New Testament often uses to describe his death can easily be misunderstood. It is metaphorical, and should not be taken in the sense that God demanded the blood of his only beloved son as the price of our salvation. God is not appeased by blood sacrifices. An emphasis on our salvation being accomplished through the bloody sacrifice of the cross is more typical of pre–Vatican II theology.

Already in the Old Testament one finds a purification of the concept of sacrifice. What God asks for is obedience, faithfulness, and a pure heart, not the blood of sacrificial animals. Thus we read in Psalms,

> Sacrifice and offering you do not desire,
> > but you have given me an open ear.
> Burnt offering and sin offering
> > you have not required.
> Then I said, "Here I am;
> > in the scroll of the book it is written of me.

> I delight to do your will, O my God;
>> your law is within my heart.
>
>>>> (Ps 40:6–8)

God does not need blood sacrifices. In language that mocks the practices of the Israelites' neighbors we read,

> Not for your sacrifices do I rebuke you;
>> your burnt offerings are continually before me.
> I will not accept a bull from your house…,

> Do I eat the flesh of bulls,
>> or drink the blood of goats?
> Offer to God a sacrifice of thanksgiving,
>> And pay your vows to the Most High.
>
>>>> (Ps 50:8–9, 13–14)

What did the paschal mystery mean for Jesus? Jesus's sacrifice was a life lived in complete union with the God he called Abba, Father. Though reviled by others, he remained gracious. Though tempted, he did not sin. His whole life was one of dying to self and living for others, seeking not his own will but the will of the one who sent him, proclaiming the reign of God even when it became evident that the opposition his preaching occasioned would eventually cost him his life. Throughout his life, evil, violence, and the demonic had no place. When treated with violence and abuse, he did not respond in kind; rather, he asked that his Father forgive those who carried out his terrible sentence. He died alone, hoping only in his Abba, crying out in his last moments, "Father, into your hands I commend my spirit" (Luke 23:46). In his Letter to the Philippians, Paul quotes an early Christian hymn to express this self-emptying pattern of Jesus's life:

> Who, though he was in the form of God,
>> did not regard equality with God
>> as something to be exploited,

but emptied himself,
　　taking the form of a slave,
　　being born in human likeness.
And being found in human form,
　　he humbled himself
　　and became obedient to the point of death—
　　even death on a cross.

(Phil 2:6–8; cf. 2 Cor 8:9)

And God raised him up, showing once and for all that God's love is stronger than death, that God does not abandon those who are faithful to him, a theme already developed in the Old Testament (Ps 16:9–11; cf. Ps 73:25–26). It is important to see that the resurrection was something that happened to Jesus; typical New Testament language is "he was raised up" or "God raised Jesus from the dead." Robert Imbelli writes that this self-emptying pattern that characterizes the historical life and ministry of Jesus "characterizes God's grace universally, wherever it is found. Whether within or outside the empirical Christian community, God's grace always bears a paschal shape."[1]

THE PASCHAL JOURNEY

New Testament images, such as taking up our cross, the seed dying before it can live and grow, sharing in Christ's death so that we might share in his resurrection, all point to Jesus's Passover from death to life as the model for our own. As the Second Vatican Council's document the Pastoral Constitution on the Church in the Modern World, *Gaudium et spes*, states, "The Holy Spirit in a manner known only to God offers to every man [or woman] the possibility of being associated with this paschal mystery" (no. 22). In his encyclical on evangelization, *Evangelii gaudium* (2013), Pope Francis touches on what is at the heart of the paschal mystery, describing it as a profound law of reality at the source of authentic human fulfillment, teaching us "that life is attained and matures in the measure that it is offered up in order to give life to others" (no. 10).

Our own participation in the paschal mystery begins with our baptism, for we are baptized into Christ's death (Rom 6:3–4). The Fourth Gospel describes baptism as a new birth in water and the Spirit. We receive the spirit of adoption as sons and daughters "when we cry, 'Abba! Father!'" (Rom 8:15), and we reproduce the pattern of Jesus's dying and rising in our own lives by living selflessly, modeling our lives on Jesus's life of faithfulness to God and service to others. This means a dying to self, to all that is not God, so that we might live in communion with God.

We remind ourselves of Christ's paschal mystery in the celebration of the Eucharist, proclaiming his death until he comes again, giving thanks for his resurrection and gift of the Holy Spirit in the great Eucharistic Prayer. The Second Vatican Council sees an intimate connection between liturgy and life. Its Constitution on the Liturgy, *Sacrosanctum concilium*, calls the faithful, filled with "the paschal sacraments," to that renewal of the covenant between the Lord and his people that draws the faithful into the compelling love of Christ (SC 10). When the Council speaks of the "fully conscious, and active participation" of the faithful in liturgical celebrations (no. 14), it means more than simply a multiplication of liturgical roles, though that is important also. The eucharistic liturgy invites us into Christ's offering of himself completely to the Father in his passage from death to life. For example, in Eucharistic Prayer II, the priest prays for a member of the community who has died:

> Remember your servant N.,
> whom you have called (today)
> from this world to yourself.
>   Grant that he (she) who was united with your Son
> in a death like his,
> may also be one with him in his Resurrection.

So Christ's paschal mystery is continued through his Body, the Church. We accompany Jesus in his passion, just as each of us must one day make that same lonely journey from life, through death, to life eternal.

In his encyclical *Laudato si'*, Francis brings all creation into the mystery of Christ's work of reconciliation, noting that in the Christian understanding of the world, the destiny of all creation is bound up with the mystery of Christ, present from the beginning. He cites Colossians 1:16 to the effect that "all things have been created through him and for him" and the Prologue of the Gospel of John, which sees Christ's creative work as the Divine Logos; he says, "One Person of the Trinity entered into the created cosmos, throwing in his lot with it, even to the cross. From the beginning of the world, but particularly through the incarnation, the mystery of Christ is at work in a hidden manner in the natural world as a whole, without thereby impinging on its autonomy" (no. 99).

This is the paschal mystery into which we were baptized. Our way there is not always easy. Certainly, Jesus's way was not, but God was with him, the God he called Abba, Father, even if the divinity hides itself in his passion, as St. Ignatius says in his *Spiritual Exercises*. And the God of Jesus will be with us also.

12

The Imitation of Christ

Closely related to the paschal mystery is the idea of the imitation of Christ (*Imitatio Christi*), traceable back to St. Paul. Stressing how his own life since his conversion has been patterned on the life of Christ, Paul writes, "I want to know Christ and the power of his resurrection and the sharing of his sufferings by becoming like him in his death, if somehow I may attain the resurrection from the dead" (Phil 3:10–11). This describes the paschal mystery, as we have seen.

MARTYRS

In the post-New Testament period, martyrdom was seen as the preeminent way of imitating Christ. The Acts of the Apostles presents an idealized picture of the death of Stephen, the first Christian martyr, who like Jesus, dies asking God to forgive his executioners (Acts 7:60). The early martyrs (the Greek *marturein* means "to witness") were honored for witnessing to the faith by their deaths. Thus, Ignatius of Antioch wrote to the Romans, beseeching them not to deprive him of the crown of martyrdom, that he might become a "true disciple" of Christ by becoming "an imitator of the passion of my God" (*The Epistle to the Romans*, no. VI). Justin Martyr, a second century philosopher turned Christian apologist, describes how the courage showed by persecuted Christians led him to the faith: "When I was a disciple of Plato," he writes, "hearing the accusations made against the Christians and seeing them intrepid in the face of death and of all that men fear, I said to myself that it was impossible that they should be living in evil and in the love of pleasure" (II Apol. 18, 1). The early Christians gathered at the tombs of the martyrs, seeing them as icons of Christ. They would ask their intercession, celebrate the Eucharist, and share a meal, a tradition inherited from pagan funeral rites, not unlike the Mexican celebration of the *Dia de los Muertos*. As the age of martyrs faded into history, others who sought a closer following or imitation of Christ left the cities for a solitary life in the desert; the monastic literature often described their life of prayer and penance as a "white" or bloodless martyrdom.

IMITATING CHRIST

In Eastern Christianity, the imitation of Christ focused on the divinity of Jesus, as Christians sought to imitate his union with God in their own lives. Little attention was paid to the humanity of Jesus. One commentator notes that Benedict, in his monastic *Rule*, referred to Jesus as a man only three times, and never used his name: "He is presented as the Lord and God and the life of a monk is one of service and devotion to him as King, Father, Good Shepherd, and Teacher."[1] From the eighth century on, crucifixes began appearing in the west, but as in the east, the figure of Jesus was portrayed as alive and triumphant, dressed in royal or priestly vesture.

By the eleventh and twelfth centuries, as the religious imagination of Christians began to focus on the humanity of Jesus, the idea of imitating Christ began to take on new meaning. Crucifixes now began to portray the suffering or dead Christ. In the writing of theologians like Anselm and Peter Damian, there was a new emphasis on the ethical character of Christianity. The twelfth-century Cistercians Aelred of Rievaulx, William of St. Thierry, and Bernard of Clairvaux encouraged the use of the imagination in contemplating the humanity of Christ, while Francis of Assisi and Clare sought to personally imitate his life of poverty and service to the poor. Ludolph of Saxony's *Vita Christi* presented some two thousand pages of meditations on the life of Christ; the focus on his life was to help one imitate him.

Thomas à Kempis's fifteenth-century work *The Imitation of Christ* was surpassed only by the Bible in popularity. A product of a movement known as the *Devotio Moderna*, the author was most probably a member of the Brethren of the Common Life, a community of priests and laity founded in the Netherlands by Geert de Groote (1340–84). The book was a practical work of piety, stressing withdrawal into an interior life modeled on the life of Jesus. Between 1470 and 1520, it appeared in more than one hundred twenty editions and seven languages.

Ignatius of Loyola read *The Imitation of Christ*, as well as Ludolph's *Vita Christi*, during his long convalescence at Loyola; these were two of the three books he had available to him. They played an important role in shaping the spirituality that would later be reflected in his *Spiritual Exercises*, especially the ideal of following the poor and humble Jesus. This comes to expression in the meditation on the Call of Christ the King (The Two Standards) and in the consideration of the Three Degrees of Humility.

Terrence Tilley gives a modern interpretation of the *Imitatio Christi* in his book on Christology, *The Disciples' Jesus*. He argues that being a disciple of Jesus meant not learning his teaching but imitating the reconciling practices of the Jesus movement; in this way, the disciples followed Jesus by living in and living out the reign of God: healing, teaching, forgiving, and sharing table fellowship. Even though the disciples were not reported in the Gospels to have engaged in the forgiveness of sins, they were involved in the practice of forgiving all that stood in the way of reconciliation. Jesus's practice of healing and exorcising restored to the community those marginalized or excluded by sickness or mental illness. Hospitality and table fellowship means "treating the stranger as guest, the Other as friend, the opponent as a colleague who differs, sometimes in important ways, from us," all of which Tilley suggests is a model for the Church today and certainly for the Christians who want to imitate Jesus in their own personal lives.[2]

CONTEMPORARY MARTYRS

Even today, martyrdom remains an extraordinary way of following or imitating Jesus, and it has by no means passed from history. Susan Bergman's book on contemporary martyrs points out that by various estimates, the twentieth century—the "tyrant century" in the words of Osip Mandelstam, martyred in Russia—has produced more Christian martyrs than all the others combined, perhaps as many as twenty-six million.[3] The early decades of the twenty-first century have produced more martyrs, Christians among them, especially in parts of the Middle East under the control of ISIS, leading Secretary of State John Kerry to speak of genocide. Bergman's book is a collection of moving portraits by contemporary writers of some of those men and women. There is much we can learn from them. Each story is unique and moving.

Simone Weil was a French activist and mystic, born of Jewish parents. Never baptized, she died at the age of thirty-four in a British sanatorium.[4] Weil teaches us the virtue of solidarity with the disadvantaged and the oppressed. Janani Luwum was the Anglican archbishop of Kampala, Uganda, tortured and killed by Idi Amin after accusing his government of the abuse of power and arbitrary bloodletting. In defying the tyrant, he teaches us courage.

Some have pushed forward the definition of martyrdom. Nate Saint, a Baptist missionary, was killed with his companions in Ecuador in 1956 as they tried to make contact with the Huaorani Indians, a story dramatized in the movie *End of the Spear*. He teaches us the cost of evangelization. Maria Goretti, a young Italian girl, was stabbed to death while resisting the sexual advances of a young neighbor. Kathleen Norris tells her story in a wonderful essay, challenging the popular picture of Maria as a martyr for chastity. Instead, she sees her as one whose particular witness was a courageous resistance to evil, combined with the ability to forgive the man who took her life as she lay dying, an act of grace that contributed ultimately to the man's conversion. She teaches us the virtue of forgiveness.

Charles de Foucauld, a former French military officer and explorer, underwent a conversion that led him ultimately to a vision of the spirituality of Jesus's hidden life at Nazareth. He sought to imitate Jesus by a life of solidarity with the impoverished Algerian Tuareg tribesmen of the Sahara. He was murdered in 1916 by a fifteen-year-old bandit in an attempted kidnapping. He inspired the Little Brothers and Little Sisters of Jesus who today seek to imitate the hidden life of Jesus at Nazareth.

As noted earlier, Oscar Romero, Archbishop of El Salvador, was assassinated in 1980 for his outspoken advocacy of the country's poor in the face of an oppressive government; he was murdered while saying Mass. In a sermon after the murder of a government minister, Romero sought to defend his socially engaged priests from the charge of being communists and at the same time renounce violence in response to the murder: "One side accuses the church of being Marxist and subversive. Another group of people wants to reduce the church to a spirituality that is separated from the realities of the world, a type of preaching that remains in the clouds, that sings the psalms and prayers, without any concern for earthly affairs."[5]

Also included are the stories of Maximilian Kolbe, the Polish Conventual Franciscan who volunteered to take the place of another prisoner (with a family) condemned to an Auschwitz death cell, and Dietrich Bonhoeffer, the German Lutheran, who was part of the anti-Hitler resistance. He was arrested by the Gestapo in April 1943. He was later found to have contacts with some members of the 20 July plot (also known as Operation Valkyrie) against Hitler in 1944. Moved from Tegel prison in Berlin to Flossenbürg concentration camp, he was executed by hanging just a few weeks before the war ended. In one of his last letters to his friend Eberhard Bethge, he said he had in the last year "come to know and understand...the profound this-worldliness of Christianity," meaning by this a life characterized by discipline and the constant knowledge of death and resurrection, even a watching with Christ in Gethsemane.[6] Other chapters include the stories of Etty Hillesum and Edith Stein, now St. Teresa Benedicta of the Cross. Their stories are among my favorites.

Edith Stein came from a Jewish family in Breslau, now Wroclaw in Poland. A brilliant young woman, she studied at Göttingen and then Freiburg under Edmund Husserl, the founder of phenomenology, becoming one of his most famous students. But she found herself drawn toward Christianity. She describes how moved she was on entering a Catholic church in Frankfurt, and seeing someone simply kneeling in silent prayer, something she didn't experience either in her Jewish experience or in Protestant churches.

After reading the life of St. Teresa of Avila (also from a Jewish family), she exclaimed, "This is the Truth." She was baptized in 1922, and after finishing her doctorate, taught for a number of years at a Dominican convent school in Speyer. In 1933, the year Hitler came to power, she entered Carmel in Cologne, unable to continue teaching in Germany because of the Nazi anti-Jewish laws excluding "non-Aryans" from professional positions. After Kristallnacht (1938), the night of the broken glass on which the Nazis attacked the Jews and trashed synagogues and Jewish shops throughout Germany, she moved to the Carmelite convent in Echt, the Netherlands, as even her presence in Cologne endangered the sisters there. Shortly after the Dutch bishops spoke out against the persecution of the Jews, the Nazis arrested all the Catholic Jews in Holland. Edith and her sister, staying at the convent in Echt, were picked up by the Gestapo on August 2, transported east, and died at Auschwitz on August 9. She was canonized on October 11, 1998, as Sr. Teresa Benedicta of the Cross, as she was known in the community.

In the final essay of Bergman's work, one of the writers quotes Pope John Paul II in a contemporary martyrology of his own composing, saying of this great multitude, "They have completed in their death as martyrs the redemptive suffering of Christ." Bergman's book is powerful because it takes seriously the efforts of each martyr portrayed to enter into his or her life fully. These were real men and women, who faced honestly the challenges that their lives brought them. Their holiness consists not in avoiding the implications of their humanity, but in embracing it, seeking to imitate the Jesus they followed.

This is the call of every Christian to face whatever difficult challenges their position or vocation brings, with its often damaged relationships, difficult choices, demand for facing problems and thinking critically, in the effort to transform all through the power of the gospel. Particularly moving is that so many saw their own suffering as a participation in the paschal mystery of Jesus, the *Imitatio Christi* to which we are all called.

PART III

THE SPIRIT

13

THE SPIRIT AND GRACE

How do we understand the Holy Spirit? We sense God's presence in the beauty of creation and sometimes as a comforting presence that fills our hearts. The Old Testament speaks of God's works, calling a people, entering into relationship with them, promising them salvation in a future rich in hope. The psalms especially celebrate what it means to live in covenant relationship with God, even if God remains mystery.

Jesus is more concrete. We can imagine him; with the help of the Gospels, we are able to contemplate the mysteries of his life. He has a voice that is often challenging; he tells us that we meet him in the poor, that as disciples we have to take up our cross and follow after him, that his greatest commandment is that we love one another, even be willing to lay down our life for another. He has a body, both eucharistic and ecclesial; in our communion in his body and blood, we become his Body for the world, the Church.

In the Old Testament, the Spirit personifies God's work, manifesting God's presence. It hovers over the primordial waters at the beginning of time, raises up the charismatic judges to defend the tribes in the land of Canaan, anoints kings, and inspires the prophets. In the New Testament, Jesus is conceived through the Holy Spirit; the Spirit comes down on him at his baptism, leads him into the desert, and empowers his ministry. He promises to send the Spirit to dwell with the disciples.

But the Spirit is difficult to imagine or describe. As Brian Daley says, the Spirit seems to lack a "face," it is "a gift, a force, but seems not to have the individual concreteness that Greek philosophy referred to by the term *hypostasis*."[1] Daley suggests that the Spirit "is simply too close to us, too much involved in our own lives of faith, to be adequately conceived or imagined."[2]

More affect than object, the Spirit is felt or discerned; it can never be controlled. In the Church's tradition, the word *grace* has been used to refer to the Spirit's presence and activity, though too often our language of *grace* made it sound like it was a thing, a mysterious something to be gained or lost. Since the Second Vatican Council, the understanding of grace has been more of a personal encounter or relationship with God. But the Spirit is more than simply a personification of God's activity. The Council of Constantinople (381) affirmed the divinity of the Spirit. It taught that the Holy Spirit, the Lord, the Giver of Life, who proceeds from the Father, with the Father and the Son is worshipped and glorified, adding that the Spirit has spoken through the prophets, pointing to the Spirit's work in history.

The Spirit is the source of our faith. St. Paul says that no one can say, "Jesus is Lord," that fundamental confession of Christian faith, except through the Holy Spirit (1 Cor 12:3). It is the Spirit that enables us to cry out, like Jesus, "Abba! Father!" (Rom 8:15). In John's Gospel, Jesus promises the disciples that he will send the Holy Spirit or "Advocate" to teach them and remind the disciples of all that he had told them (John 14:26). In some of the great religious autobiographies—for example, Thomas Merton's *The Seven Storey Mountain*, Dorothy Day's *The Long Loneliness*, or James Martin's *In Good Company: The Fast Track from the Corporate World to Poverty, Chastity, and Obedience*—one senses the Spirit leading the author to faith, thus being at work in the person's life even prior to baptism.

The Spirit is also the source of the life and unity of the Church. It is the Spirit of God that animates the Church. Paul teaches us that the Church is a "temple sacred in the Lord; in him you also are being built together into a dwelling place of God in the Spirit" (Eph 2:21–22, NABRE), equipped with a diversity of gifts and ministries (1 Cor 12:4–11; cf. Rom 12:4–8). The Spirit is also the source of the Church's unity. According to Paul, "For in the one Spirit we were all baptized into one body—Jews or Greeks, slaves or free—and we were all made to drink of one Spirit" (1 Cor 12:13). Thus, the Spirit's role is to break down divisions, uniting the baptized in Christ so that for those—using a lovely metaphor—who have been "clothed" with Christ, "there is no longer Jew or Greek, there is no longer slave or free, there is no longer male and female; for all of you are one in Christ Jesus" (Gal 3:27–28). The Second Vatican Council teaches that all the faithful, ordained and lay, share in the threefold office of Christ as prophet, priest, and king (LG 31) and all are called to holiness.

But Christians have often been slow to fully grasp the meaning of this unity in Christ, with its implication of breaking down divisions based on confession, ethnicity, race, social status, gender, or sexual orientation. The early Church struggled long over its relationship to Israel; while Christianity and Judaism had emerged as separate religions by the end of the first century, both communities were unable to recognize each other as belonging to God's people, even if they worshiped the same God in different ways. The sorry history of Christian anti-Judaism and even anti-Semitism continued down to modern times.

Nor was the early Church able to challenge the institution of slavery on which so much of the ancient world was built; while it sought to change the relationships between masters and slaves, as the Letter to Philemon gives witness, the Church tolerated slavery, even by Christians, for centuries. Various popes condemned the slave trade from the fifteenth century down to the nineteenth, but their teaching was largely ignored by bishops, clergy, and laity. Prior to the Civil War, some bishops tried to argue that this papal teaching did not apply to the situation in the United States, and even the Jesuits were slow to speak out against it, some actually owning slaves.[3] In 1838, Georgetown University sold

272 slaves—men, women, and children—to help meet the struggling college's financial obligations.

And there are other divisions in the Body of Christ. Many would argue that the Church has been slow to recognize the full equality of men and women in the Church. Others struggle to more adequately recognize the dignity of the LGBTQ community. And the Church itself is divided into different communities and churches, no longer in communion with each other.

Finally, the Spirit gives us a share in the inner life of God. At the Last Supper, Jesus promised his disciples that he would not leave them orphans, assuring them that he would send the Advocate or Spirit to be with them always, and that he and the Father would dwell within them: "Those who love me will keep my word, and my Father will love them, and we will come to them and make our home with them" (John 14:23). To live in the Spirit, to live in God's grace, is to participate in God's triune life. Karl Rahner, especially, has stressed that grace is God's free self-communication, God's indwelling, enabling, salvific presence, offered to all, though it must be freely accepted. Vatican II broke new ground in affirming this, teaching that God's salvific grace is available even to those who do not know Christ or his Church, though some succumb to the temptations of the evil one, exchanging the truth of God for a lie and serving the creature rather than the Creator (LG 16).

Contemporary theology is reclaiming the connection between the Trinity and the doctrine of creation; it sees God's grace or Spirit as present and active in our world, giving it life, reflecting the goodness and beauty of the Creator. The medieval distinction between the natural and supernatural orders makes little sense today; there never has been a world without grace. Indeed, the Spirit of God is to be found at the heart of the evolutionary process that has shaped and continues to shape our world, calling us in the great drama of life to a future union with God when God will be all in all (1 Cor 15:28). The tragedy of evolutionary materialists is that they can see no room for God or God's Spirit; they reduce the incredible story of life in all its richness and diversity to a mechanism, a series of accidents, random occurrences leading nowhere.

But those able to see with the eyes of faith have a richer view. In language at once theological and poetic, Elizabeth Johnson seeks to integrate the theory of evolution with Christian faith. Speaking of God's Spirit with maternal metaphors, she writes, "Neither overriding monarch nor absent deist god, the Spirit of God moves with extravagant divine generosity to create and sustain the conditions that have enabled the biodiverse community of life to become so interesting and beautiful. The unimaginable epochs of time over which this has occurred are themselves a gift of opportunity for nature's emergent freedom to work."[4]

Eastern Christianity has traditionally paid more attention to the place of the Spirit in liturgy and life, while the focus of Western Christianity has been more christological, at the expense of pneumatology. The amazing growth of Pentecostal communities today has led some to speak of a third wave in the history of the Church.[5] If the first wave is represented by the historic churches of the first millennium, the second wave is constituted by the Reformation churches, while the third wave is made up of the Evangelical, charismatic, and above all, Pentecostal communities. Pentecostal Christians grew from 74 million in 1970 to an estimated 497 million by 1997, an increase of 670 percent. Estimates of all those associated with Pentecostalism range from 500 to 600 million, close to 25 percent of the world's Christians.

St. Irenaeus was accustomed to speak of the "two hands of the Father," the Son and the Spirit who make discernible God's work and presence in history.[6] The multiplication of Pentecostal churches should serve as a reminder to the more traditional churches not to forget the place of the Spirit. At the same time, Christology cannot be replaced by pneumatology. The two are inseparable.

14

SPIRITUALITY

Some religious sociologists and spiritual writers are beginning to critique the often fuzzy, uncritical concepts of spirituality, disconnected from religious traditions, so popular today. Robert Wuthnow, perhaps the premiere sociologist of religion currently in the United States, is one of them. He writes, "The idea that spirituality is being pursued outside of organized religion is both plausible and worrisome."[1] This is especially true of young adults today, particularly those who proclaim, "I'm spiritual but not religious."

So what is spirituality? Etymologically derived from the Latin *spiritus* and *spiritualis* and used to translate Paul's *pneuma* and *pneumatikos*, *spiritual* carries the sense of being open to or guided by the Spirit, as opposed to one who is "carnal," driven by the needs of the flesh. Saying that "we have not received the spirit of the world but the Spirit that is from God, so that we may understand the things freely given us by God," Paul contrasts the spiritual person with the natural, the one who does not accept what comes from the Spirit of God (1 Cor 2:12, 14, NABRE). Thus, a Christian spirituality is a way of organizing one's life in openness to the Spirit; it includes certain gospel values, methods of prayer, worship, and a disciplined way of living as a disciple of Jesus. Its goal is a growth in union with God, in a word, *holiness.*

Wuthnow wonders how one can effectively measure people's

interest in spirituality, when spirituality itself can mean so many different things. Much of it seems irrational, based on self-indulgent fantasizing, or essentially private, personally invented sets of beliefs and practices. When books like *Chicken Soup for the Soul* and *The Celestine Prophecy* can pass for spirituality, serious observers of American religion are concerned "because they provide ready-made answers for the small setbacks and petty anxieties of ordinary life but do not speak of a righteous God who demands anything of believers."[2]

SPIRITUAL BUT NOT RELIGIOUS

Wuthnow notes that among those who say that spirituality is fairly important, three quarters do not attend religious services regularly and half are not church members. Thus, questions could be raised about the seriousness of their spiritual commitment. He argues that "people with the highest commitment to spiritual growth are overwhelmingly involved in religious organizations: eighty percent of those who value spiritual growth the most are church members, and seventy-one percent say they attend worship services almost every week."[3]

In an article titled "Religion vs. Spirituality: A Contemporary Conundrum," Sandra Schneiders argues that a "non-religious spirituality" reflects a postmodern mentality, whereas religions like Christianity presuppose a unitary worldview. A nonreligious spirituality "is usually a privatized, idiosyncratic, personally satisfying stance and practice which makes no doctrinal claims, imposes no moral authority outside one's own conscience, creates no necessary personal relationships or social responsibilities, and can be changed or abandoned whenever it seems not to work for the practitioner."[4]

In Vincent Miller's book *Consuming Religion*, he warns that such self-constructed spiritualties, shaped by the habits of our consumer-driven society, transform even the religious values we profess. Consumption becomes the dominant cultural practice, though he also points out that a consumer culture is experienced by many as liberating, allowing people to construct their own identities, freeing them from cultural constraints, external authorities, and predetermined gender and social roles.[5] This needs to be acknowledged, even if the trend remains problematic.

Nevertheless, this "commodification" of religion reduces the riches of our religious traditions to images, symbols, music, paraphernalia, practices, and personalities from which seekers can select, and it deprives them of their ability to shape daily life. Spirituality becomes disconnected from religion, while the "stuff" of religion, its appropriated symbols and practices, are separated from their original liturgical, communal, and institutional contexts that secured their meanings. Religious traditions become repositories of interesting objects for personal choice, such as rosaries hanging from a rearview mirror but never prayed. The result is the privatization of religion. Perhaps this explains the popularity of Joseph Campbell, who has made widely available symbols and practices from the world religions, but stripped them from their communal and institutional contexts so that they can be appropriated by individuals into their own private religions or spiritualties.

Miller speaks of this as the "deregulation" of religion, freeing it from the tradition in which it has been embedded and liberating it from its authority. While he does not see this as necessarily negative or that spiritualties personally chosen, like commodities, are necessarily shallow, he argues that spirituality needs communal support if it is to be more than sentiment. When religious beliefs and practices are abstracted from the cultures, institutions, and relationships in which they were once embedded, they can no longer inform the shape of daily life: "Commitments to visions of the spiritual life, no matter how profound, are difficult to sustain without a community of shared belief. Furthermore, if religious syntheses are to inform the practice of daily life, they require some articulation in discipline and practices. This again is difficult to achieve on the individual level."[6]

One way to counter the commodification of religion is to stress engagement in the liturgical, the sacramental, and the ecclesial. The Church lives from a tradition reaching back to the earliest Christian communities; it mediates a faith that is essentially public, not private.

Sacraments are coded by that tradition. Scripture is read from a lectionary shared by a global Church; it is not chosen on the basis of personal preference. As Miller says, in the liturgy, "one is not free to yawn and move on to a more interesting passage, or to decide that it is irrelevant."[7]

A TRANSFORMATIVE SPIRITUALITY

So how can we help others come to those transformative experiences like Moses before the burning bush (Exod 3:2), like Jesus at his baptism (Mark 1:9–11), or Paul on the road to Damascus (Acts 9:1–9)? How can we help them, especially our young people, many of whom are drawn to service, to move beyond the self-chosen, culturally determined spiritualties of *Chicken Soup for the Soul* and discover the face of Jesus? How can we help them to recognize the presence of the God who inspires their generosity? God, of course, remains mystery. We cannot engineer such an encounter so that it happens in a place we have chosen or on a schedule we have determined. We can only be witnesses, mediators, and fellow pilgrims. But there are things we can do.

First, be honest, and be willing to share your own experience. Personal witness or testimony is important to young people. Pope Paul VI was well aware of this. In his great apostolic exhortation on evangelization, *Evangelii nutiandi*, he wrote, "Modern man listens more willingly to witness than to teachers, and if he does listen to teachers, it is because they are witnesses" (no. 41). As we have seen, Andrew Greeley continually reminded us that the tradition of the Church, what he liked to call our "Catholic religious sensibility," is passed on first of all by parents and spouses and by telling stories.[8] He contrasted this "popular tradition" with the "high tradition" contained in the teaching of theologians and the magisterium. We need to be willing to tell our own stories and those of our own mentors in the faith. Stories, especially personal ones, engage us; they embody values and draw us in.

Second, don't be judgmental. We need to speak the truth in addressing issues of faith and theology, but to do so in a nonthreatening way. Part of the relativism of contemporary culture as well as the pluralism and celebration of diversity that characterizes higher education today is an allergic reaction to anything that sounds judgmental. How can one religious view be better than another? Aren't they all good? So tolerance becomes the highest virtue. What gets lost is the very possibility of truth. Cardinal Carlo Martini characterizes this postmodern mentality as preferring beauty to truth. "There is acceptance of every form of dialogue and exchange because of a desire to be always open to another and to what is different."[9]

Third, emphasize experience. Religious commentators like Philip Jenkins identify Pentecostalism as perhaps the most successful social movement of the past century with the potential to surpass the one billion mark before 2050.[10] While this growth has taken place chiefly in the Southern Hemisphere, there is a lesson to be learned from it for global Christianity.

In a perceptive comment, the late Renato Poblete, a Chilean Jesuit, attributed the effectiveness of the Pentecostals to their emphasis on a personal experience of God, something he says has long been lost sight of in western theology.[11] Poblete's Jesuit tradition privileges experience. Just as he stressed the importance of the imagination in prayer, in his *Spiritual Exercises*, Ignatius of Loyola frequently used the Spanish verbs *gustar* (to taste) and *sentir* (to experience, to perceive through the senses) to emphasize a knowledge rooted in experience. The second annotation at the beginning of the *Exercises* says that "it is not abundance of knowledge that fills and satisfies the soul, but the inward sense (*sentir*) and taste (*gustar*) of things."

Pope Francis shows this same Ignatian sensibility in his appreciation for traditional piety or popular religion (*religiosidad popular* in the Spanish), with its emphasis on feeling or sentiment. Faith, he says, is ruled by sentiments (*sentimientos*) of the heart that lead to prayer and service. He appeals to John of the Cross, Teresa of Avila, and Ignatius himself to show that sentiment is not incompatible with deep spiritual experience. These Spanish mystics and reformers stress the affective side of faith. Francis values traditional piety because it touches the heart, entering into the daily life of the people.[12] Thus affectivity is not antithetical to critical thinking, but often the path to insight and understanding. We need to appeal both to the head and to the heart.

The present interest in spirituality, if properly guided, could be a rich resource for helping young adults gain some insight into the Divine Mystery, even to come to know the transcendent God who has chosen to enter into a relationship with humankind historically, first through the prophets and teachers of Israel and their Scriptures, and finally through the Word become flesh, Jesus. But they will need others to accompany them, mentors and guides, men and women, whose own lives have been enriched by their faith and who are willing to share their experience with others.

15

THE POWER OF COMPASSION

Acouple of years ago, I was rushing through Los Angeles International Airport, hoping to grab a quick coffee and a scone at Starbucks before my flight. But as I entered the American Airlines concourse, what I saw was not the famous Seattle coffee concession but a Homegirl Café, busy with several Mexican American girls waiting on the early morning commuters. Gosh, I thought to myself, Greg has created a whole industry!

GREG BOYLE

Greg is Fr. Greg Boyle, a Jesuit brother and friend, a few years behind me in the Society, known to all of Los Angeles and far beyond for his work with the "homies," the homeboys and homegirls whose lives and bodies have been so marked by the culture of violence that is the gang life of East L.A. Greg grew up in Los Angeles, the gang capital of the world, but in a very different, decidedly middle-class neighborhood. He entered the Society of Jesus in 1972 and was ordained in 1984. Originally scheduled for ministry at one of our universities, after Spanish language studies in Bolivia and daily contact with the country's poor, he asked to be assigned to Dolores Mission, the poorest parish in the Archdiocese of Los Angeles in the midst of two large housing projects and some eight gangs. He was then the youngest pastor in the archdiocese.

Realizing how many young lives were blunted by the gangs, he began by riding his bike through the neighborhood in the evenings, trying to get to know the young people. At first they ignored him; they saw him as an interloper or "do-gooder." But gradually, as he visited them in jails or hospitals, they realized he was there for them. They started calling him "G," for Greg, or "G-Dog." In 1988, he buried his first victim of gang violence. Twenty years later, he had presided at over 165 such funerals for young men from the neighborhood. His book *Tattoos on the Heart: The Power of Boundless Compassion*[1] is a *New York Times* best seller, and named one of the Best Books of 2010 by *Publishers Weekly*. It is the story of his efforts to provide jobs as a way out of gang life for these young men and women through Homeboy Industries. As he likes to say, "Nothing stops a bullet like a job."

Homeboy Industries began when a Hollywood agent came to see Greg after the death of his wife, wanting to do something to address the growing gang problem. After shooting down a number of his suggestions, none of them practical, Boyle suggested that the agent buy an old bakery for sale in the neighborhood; he would try to bring rival gang members together to work with each other in what he would call The Homeboy Bakery. Soon he had gang members arriving, looking for a job. One of them, just released from prison, arrived with "FUCK THE WORLD" tattooed on his forehead. Imagining him trying to get a job at McDonalds and scaring away the customers, one of Greg's first services was a tattoo removal program.

GREG'S STORIES

The stories in the book break one's heart. There was Jason, a young crack dealer, the son of two addicts. After rejecting a number of invitations, Jason finally showed up at Greg's office and, with his help, found a job. Having left his anger behind, he eventually found himself a home and family, and was looking forward to his daughter's baptism. He had bought her a new dress. A week before the baptism, he was gunned down in the streets by someone from his past. Then there is Luis, also a drug dealer, one of the biggest and smartest in the community, who for years had avoided the law. After his daughter, Tiffany, was born, he too came to Greg, was hired to work at the bakery and with his natural leadership ability was soon appointed foreman. He took being a father seriously, got a small apartment, the first home he had ever had, and with it a whole new life. One evening while loading his car, he too was shot and killed by some gang members who found themselves in his neighborhood. As Greg said at his funeral, Luis "had come to know the truth about himself and liked what he found there."

There are too many stories like those of Jason and Luis, kids who Greg befriended, young men who, through unconditional love and care, discovered the truth about themselves, turned their lives around, rejoiced in their children, and looked to a future with hope. They came from broken homes and abusive, addicted, or absent parents—dysfunctional families. Lacking love and self-respect, they were burdened with shame that was situational as well as personal. You find yourself identifying with them, marveling at their humor, their resiliency, only to have them end up one more victim of the violence of the streets. Like the sixteen-year-old girl, pregnant, who says to Greg, "I just want to have a kid before I die." Or Benito, a funny energetic twelve-year-old killed in a drive-by. Many do turn their lives around. Those stories are there too.

My favorite is about Bandit, well named for "being at home in all things illegal." He came to see Greg after a lot of time locked up for selling crack. Greg took him to a job developer, who got him an unskilled, entry-level job at a warehouse. Fifteen years later, he visits Greg; he now runs the warehouse, has his own home, a wife, and three kids. He wants Greg to bless his oldest daughter; she's not in trouble, but is going to college, the first in her family to do so, and wants to study forensic psychology. Greg tells Bandit how proud he is of him, who answers with tears in his eyes, "I'm proud of myself. All my life, people called me a lowlife, a *bueno para nada*. I guess I showed them." Greg calls this the slow work of God,[2] helping the soul to feel its worth. It is the strategy of Jesus, not centered on taking the right stand, but rather on standing in the right place—with the outcasts and those relegated to the margins.

TATTOOS ON THE HEART

Fr. Boyle is an acute observer; he writes with a poetic sense, an ear for dialogue, and an eye for detail. The book's title comes from a moment when he complemented a homie, trying to get him to see the goodness within; the kid responded, "Damn, G...I'm going to tattoo that on my heart." The book's subtitle, *The Power of Boundless Compassion*, is what he offers. Bringing enemies together in the bakery, they work side by side each other and become friends, breaking down the illusion of separateness to replace it with kinship. Boyle finds the holy in the comic and the ordinary. He meets people who are living heroic lives, like the mother of Rigo, who every Sunday takes seven buses to visit him in prison while he serves his time. Rigo's father used to beat him, once with a pipe.

Boyle brings a depth of spiritual wisdom to the book, citing saints and mystics of the Christian tradition and his own rich insight. He writes about a God who loves us passionately, about the shame and "dis-grace" that cripples so many young people growing up in poverty and violence, and the toxic effects of neglect. In a course he taught at Folsom Prison, none of the inmates could define *compassion*, until one old-timer said, "That's what Jesus did. I mean, Compassion...IS... God." He writes about giving young people time to do the slow work of finding themselves, and about the slow work of God. His topics include gladness and joy, kinship, and success, which so often we turn into an idol. For those of us driven by the need to be successful, he quotes Mother Teresa who once said, "We are not called to be successful, but faithful." To this Greg adds, with genuine humility, "If you surrender your need for results and outcomes, success becomes God's business. I find it hard enough to just be faithful."

From its original location in the old bakery building, Homeboy Industries has grown to an 8.5-million-dollar glass and concrete headquarters in a gang neutral location on the edge of Chinatown. It houses Homeboy Bakery, a beautiful Homegirl Café along with a catering service, various craft industries, and a Homeboy Diner at City Hall. It currently employs two hundred fifty to three hundred former gang members, while some one thousand from the community take advantage of its services each month, including five hundred monthly treatments at its clinic for tattoo removal.

The stories in his book, told originally in Fr. Boyle's homilies at Mass in some twenty-five detention centers, probation camps, and juvenile facilities scattered around Los Angeles, brought tears to my eyes numerous times, as they will to yours. This is a holy book about the power of unconditional love and compassion, about the slow work of God.

16

RECONCILIATION

In his Second Letter to the Corinthians, St. Paul says that God has reconciled us to himself through Christ and given us a ministry of reconciliation. What do we understand by reconciliation? Reconciliation is central to Jesus's ministry. It means bringing together those who had been estranged, overcoming barriers, healing wounds, and restoring to friendship. Reconciliation is the work of the Spirit; it reveals the Spirit's presence. The Second Eucharistic Prayer for Reconciliation expresses this beautifully:

> By your Spirit you move human hearts
> that enemies may speak to each other again,
> adversaries join hands,
> and people seek to meet together.
> By the working of your power
> it comes about, O Lord,
> that hatred is overcome by love,
> revenge gives way to forgiveness,
> and discord is changed to mutual respect.

THE PRODIGAL SON

Luke's story of the Prodigal Son (Luke 15:11–32) is a classic story of reconciliation. The younger son asks his father for his share in the inheritance to come to him, in other words, what he would inherit after his father's death. When his father obliges him, he sets off for a distant country where he squanders his inheritance, ending up tending pigs on another man's farm, longing to eat what they are eating. Coming to his senses, he resolves to return to his home and ask his father to treat him as one of his hired hands. His father sees him while still a long way off, rushes to meet him, embraces and kisses him, and orders his servants to prepare a feast to welcome him home.

A discordant note is struck by the older brother, who resents the celebration of the prodigal's return and complains to his father about what he considers his own unrewarded service. The father assures him of his appreciation for his faithfulness, but tells him that they must celebrate and rejoice "because this brother of yours was dead and has come to life; he was lost and has been found" (v. 32).

Like all the parables, the story is rich on many levels. The father represents our merciful God who longs for the return of the sinner. Pope Francis likes to call it the story of the Prodigal Father, so lavish is God's mercy. In Rembrandt's famous representation of the scene, the son is portrayed on his knees, one shoe off, with the father's two hands wrapped around his back, one the strong hand of a male, the other more feminine, with long slender fingers, symbolizing both the father's strength and his tender, even maternal, love. Too often we find ourselves identifying not with the prodigal son, but with the elder brother, unable to share his father's joy. Reconciliation is not always easy; it demands a change of heart.

A WORLD DIVIDED

How much we need reconciliation today! When we let our imagination circle the globe, what do we see? So much violence, terrorism, war, crushing poverty, so many disadvantaged or left out of the prosperity others take for granted. So many are the victims of conflicts based in an unyielding religious fundamentalism, violence that affects members of all religions—Buddhists, Muslims, Hindus, Jews, and Christians, both Catholic and Protestant. Christians may be the most persecuted religious group today, but they are not the only one. Yazidis face near extinction in Syria and Iraq. Christians experience violence in Pakistan, often falsely accused under so-called antiblasphemy laws, with many murdered even before their trials. In India, right-wing Hindu nationalists have targeted Christians and Muslims, burning churches and mosques, beating or killing their members. Even nuns have been raped and murdered. Yet few, if any, have been arrested. In Myanmar (Burma), Buddhists have made the Rohingya, a Muslim ethnic group present there for over one thousand, what *The Economist* described as the "most persecuted people on earth." Shiites and Sunni Muslims persecute each other throughout the Middle East, while terrorist organizations claiming Muslim inspiration have driven from their homes, abused, or killed thousands in Syria, Iraq, Yemen, Somalia, Sudan, and Nigeria. Religious persecution, war, human rights violations, and crushing poverty have all contributed to the enormous number of refugees, which reached in 2013 as high as 232 million.

In many countries, democracy is only a fiction; corruption reigns, rulers change constitutional protocols to remain in power. Some countries remain to this day incapable of democratic elections; they are still ruled by centuries-old tribal factionalisms. Even in the United States, electoral districts are gerrymandered to favor one party over another, while political debates too often become live entertainment, descending into insult and name-calling, even vulgarity.

Reconciliation continues to be needed within the Church. When the film *Spotlight* won an academy award in 2016 for best picture, it brought to light again the tragic story of the Boston archdiocese's failure to deal with the sexual abuse of children and adolescents, moving offending priests to other parishes and paying the families of victims to buy their silence. The film, carefully crafted and beautifully acted, was painful to watch; but it was a story that had to be told. Even conservative Catholic papers, always sensitive to whatever might appear as Catholic "bashing," gave it good reviews.

Often our families need reconciliation. We experience some of the most meaningful moments in our families, and sometimes the most damaging. Divorce and remarriage can leave painful wounds. Gay and lesbian children are sometimes rejected. Misunderstandings or personal injuries are magnified into lasting estrangements. Some family members refuse to meet or speak to each other.

MOVING TOWARD RECONCILIATION

Reconciliation demands that someone take the first step, to reach out and extend a hand. One contemporary example comes from South Africa after the long, bloody struggle against apartheid ended with the abolition of apartheid in the early 1990s. The country established a Truth and Reconciliation Commission that invited victims of gross violations of their human rights to give public testimony about their experience, often at public hearings. At the same time, those accused of violence against others could petition for amnesty from both civil and criminal prosecution, as long as their crimes were politically motivated, proportionate, and fully disclosed. To avoid favoring only the victors in the struggle, no side was exempt from appearing before the Commission.

The Commission approved 849 amnesty applications out of some 5,392 petitions. The process was not entirely successful; some famous crimes, such as the murder of activist Steve Bilko by security police, were never justly resolved. Nevertheless, many found it a helpful way of dealing with political change after a long civil conflict, and the process was imitated by other countries. A similar process was established in Rwanda in 1999 after almost a million were killed in that country's 1994 genocide in a country where Hutus and Tutsis still live side by side. Those in jail for crimes were required to plead guilty and ask pardon of their victims.

Some of their stories are heartbreaking, told and illustrated in an online *New York Times* magazine with pictures of various couples whose not-always-smiling faces suggest how difficult the process of reconciliation actually is. Typical is the story of François and Epiphanie. François admitted that he participated in the 1994 genocide and took part in the killing of Epiphanie's son. When he came and asked for her pardon, she granted it, because as she said, he did not do it by himself and was haunted by the devil. She was pleased that he was willing to testify to the crime, instead of hiding it, saying that it hurts if someone keeps hiding a crime he committed against you. While Epiphanie had once treated him like an enemy, she says now she would rather treat him like her own child. François tells how the two of them are now members of the same reconciliation group: "We share in everything: if she needs some water to drink, I fetch some for her. There is no suspicion between us, whether under sunlight or during the night. I used to have nightmares, recalling the sad events I have been through, but now I can sleep peacefully. And when we are together, we are like brother and sister, no suspicion between us."[1]

An important prison ministry today is done by those working for "restorative justice." Based on a theory of justice that sees crimes as offenses against individuals and communities rather than the state, the process brings victims together with offenders, even violent ones. The victims are brought into dialogue with those responsible for the offense or injury, while the latter are encouraged to acknowledge the harm they have done and make amends by apologizing, making restitution, or doing community service. Bringing both parties together often proves to be both healing and highly effective. With a number of colleagues and friends involved in this ministry, I have been personally moved to witness both parties telling their stories, often in tears.

We all have need of reconciliation at different times in our lives. It begins by taking the first step, acknowledging responsibility where necessary and being willing to extend a hand in forgiveness. Each of us can ask ourselves the following: Are we willing to forgive those in our families who have injured us? Can we work for reconciliation in our communities? Are we willing to forgive the Church for its sins and failings? Can we also forgive ourselves?

Most of all, we need to remember that we are all sinners who have been forgiven by a merciful Father, reconciled through the death and resurrection of Jesus, and made one Body in Christ. For Catholics, reconciliation is a sacrament. In his travels, Pope Francis has constantly called for reconciliation, in the Central African Republic between Christians and the Muslim minority; in Nigeria with "those who might be unfriendly, even hostile, to us"; in Sarajevo, the capital of Bosnia and Herzegovina, divided along ethnic and religious lines; and for reconciliation between Catholics and Russian Orthodox in his historic 2016 meeting with Patriarch Kirill in Cuba. Francis has been willing to take the first step. We should try to do so also.

17

SALVATION

I came that they may have life, and have it abundantly.

—John 10:10

In popular American culture, heavily influenced by Evangelical Protestantism, the term *salvation* has all too often been reduced to "being saved," which in turn is understood as having been born again, freed from one's sins, and thus gaining access to eternal life in heaven. Even Catholics tend to understand salvation this way. But this is a thin concept of salvation. Biblical salvation is far richer. It is the fruit of the Spirit's work, bringing us into relation with God, ultimately to see God face-to-face (1 Cor 13:12).

SCRIPTURE

The Hebrew word *salvation* derives from the Hebrew root *YS*, which connotes open space, security, freedom from constriction; in the Old Testament, it usually means God's intervention in history on behalf of his people, Israel. The supreme example is the exodus, the deliverance of the people from slavery and oppression in Egypt under the Pharaohs.

Salvation thus is something that God has done for Israel in the past, delivering them from bondage, leading them out of Egypt, entering into covenant relationship with them on Mount Sinai, and bringing them into the promised land.

With the prophets, as they preached against the people's idolatry, disregard for the covenant, trampling on the poor, and trusting in military might rather than in Yahweh, there is a shift in the religious imagination of the people. They begin to look for a new intervention of God on their behalf, a Messiah or future Davidic king, a day of the Lord when God would come to judge with justice, a renewed or new covenant, or a reuniting of Israel and Judah through the mysterious figure of the Servant of Yahweh. The prophetic books are rich in this eschatological hope in God's coming salvation. Second Isaiah proclaims, "Do not remember the former things, / or consider the things of old. / I am about to do a new thing" (Isa 43:18–19).

For most of the Old Testament period, there was no belief in life beyond the grave, aside from a variant tradition surfacing in the psalms that God will not abandon the righteous to Sheol, the land of the dead (Pss 16:10–11; 73:26). It is only very late in Old Testament history, during the persecution of the Jews under Antiochus IV, when Jews were dying for their faithfulness to the covenant, that the idea of the resurrection of the dead enters the tradition. It comes only as a hope in a future saving act of God, that the God who created the heavens and the earth might also give life to the dead, and it was a hope, not in the resurrection of the individual, but that God would raise all the just to life in some apocalyptic moment, revealing a new order transcending the present.

This hope can be found in the Book of Daniel (12:1–3), in 2 Maccabees (7:9, 14; 12:44–45), in what is most probably a later addition to Isaiah (26:19), and in some of the late noncanonical Jewish writings. We see in the New Testament evidence that the Pharisees believed in the resurrection of the dead, while the more traditional Sadducees did not (Luke 20:27–40). Joseph Ratzinger notes a growing awareness in the Old Testament that communion with God is stronger than death

(Pss 16:9–11; 73:24–26). Also the very late Book of Wisdom, written about fifty years before the time of Jesus, expresses the beautiful idea that the souls of the just are in the hands of God (Wis 3:1–9), as we have seen.

The name *Jesus*, formed from the Hebrew root *YS*, means "Yahweh saves." The early Christians believed that God's salvation had been revealed in his life, preaching of the reign of God, his death, his resurrection, and his promise to come again, and faithful to his preaching, they understood that salvation always included justice for the poor. When they celebrated the Eucharist, they prayed for his Parousia or second coming, bringing the fullness of salvation, crying out *Marana tha*, Come, Lord (1 Cor 16:22; Rev 22:20) and facing to the East to welcome him, when, like the rising sun, he would come in glory.

SALVATION AND GRACE

What does salvation mean for us today? For many Christians, salvation means our personal hope of eternal life, of heaven, as we saw earlier. But for many others today, salvation is not a meaningful concept. Few take the Creed's confession of the resurrection of the dead seriously. Some subscribe to a popular notion that the soul or spirit lives on, or that good people go to heaven when they die even if God is not particularly involved in their lives. A relationship with God is not seen as important.

A richer concept sees salvation as God's transforming grace, present everywhere. Grace is God's healing, sustaining presence. This was the message of Jesus in his ministry; he proclaimed the joyful news ("gospel") that God's reign was at hand, evident in his ministry; he brought God's saving power into people's lives in driving out evil spirits, curing the sick, proclaiming good news to the poor and the forgiveness of sins, and reconciling to the community those who had been marginalized by religious authorities, illness, or sin. Pope Francis continues to stress that God's forgiveness is greater than our sins. God raises us up when we stumble, just as a parent raises a child who falls down.

Andrew Greeley has written that for the Catholic imagination, the world is an enchanted place with abundant opportunities for salvation, that grace is everywhere, that it can be found even in limitation, fragility, and mortality.[1] Grace can also be described as the Holy Spirit giving us a share in God's own life; it is ours through faith, and we can bring this transforming power of grace into the lives of others when we care for one another with love and compassion.

While Christianity celebrates the presence of grace, its presence is not always revealed religiously; one does not have to open the Bible or kneel in prayer or confess Jesus as Lord to experience God's grace, though of course grace can be present in those moments also. But grace is also reflected in nature, in art and literature, in symbol and story, in the stories of the saints, and the example of important people in our lives.

If God has taken on flesh in Jesus, then materiality itself is in some way sacred. Indeed, our world can mediate the divine, even in all its messiness, its family crises, its sorrows, and its pains. In Greeley's words, the world is full of grace in the ordinary events of our lives. Creation itself is revelatory; it is sacramental. The transcendent God is not distant. In his long literary career, with over two hundred books to his credit, Greeley turned from writing on sociology and theology to writing novels, rightly convinced that stories can communicate the mysterious workings of grace even better than theology. For God's grace works in and through us; it works in the ordinary events of our lives.

One example of such grace is illustrated in Tim Robbins's fine film *Dead Man Walking*, staring Susan Sarandon and Sean Penn. The movie is the story of Sr. Helen Prejean, beautifully portrayed by Sarandon, who ministers to prisoners on death row and their families, and her relationship with a condemned prisoner, played by Sean Penn. Penn's character, Matthew Poncelet, has committed a terrible crime, brutalizing a teenage couple, raping the girl, then murdering her and her boyfriend. Poncelet is a hard case; he shows no remorse, indeed seems incapable of any emotion but anger. But Sr. Helen befriends him, visiting him against the advice of others, trying to show him that someone cares for him. She becomes his friend and spiritual advisor, telling him that he must take responsibility for his crime if he is to find forgiveness. He resists, blaming others. But just before his execution, he asks the boy's father for forgiveness and expresses the hope to the parents of the girl that his death will give them some relief. His last words are that all killing is wrong—his, the government's, no matter who does it. Though the film does not show him asking God for pardon, the viewer has a clear sense that he has opened himself to grace, that God has touched him through the care that Sr. Helen has shown him.

Another powerful film is Clint Eastwood's *Gran Torino*. Eastwood plays the main character, Walt Kowalski, a retired autoworker, scarred by his experience in the Korean War and alienated from his own family. Living on beef jerky and beer after the death of his wife because he never learned to cook, and resisting the efforts of his son to find for him some assisted living, he is angry, isolated, and racist. His only friend seems to be his dog, Daisy, and his barber. When a Hmong family moves in next door, he is openly contemptuous, chasing them off his lawn and referring to them with racist epithets. The family's teenage son, Thao, under pressure from a neighborhood Hmong gang led by a cousin, tries to steal Kowalski's car, his prize Gran Torino that he helped assemble, only to be caught in the act by Kowalski. Later, when the gang returns to attack Thao, he drives them off with his M1 rifle, with the result that the family begins to see him in a new light.

Thao's mother arranges for him to work for Walt, who resists the idea at first, and he continues to insult the boy, but gradually he takes an interest in him, teaching him how to use his tools and giving him some for himself. He also gives this shy, hesitant young man some fatherly advice about dating. At the same time, Thao's older sister, Sue, sees through Walt's tough façade to his loneliness, and invites him to a family feast. Kowalski goes only because he is out of beer, and Sue tells him that they have plenty. He finds the food delicious, and soon other members of the Hmong community begin bringing him dishes they have prepared. After the gang confronts Thao coming home from work and beats him up, Kowalski goes to their house and knocks one of the gang members down as a warning. In retaliation, the gang does a drive by shooting on Thao's house; they also kidnap and rape his sister, Sue. Though Sue is badly hurt, no one in the community will testify against the gang, so Thao decides to take revenge himself, asking Walt for help.

Walt says to come back in the late afternoon. With a plan in mind, he buys a new suit, gets a haircut, and goes to confession, something his wife had asked the young Polish curate to arrange, only to be repeatedly rebuffed by Walt. When Thao shows up, Walt locks him in his basement, telling him that one does not easily get over killing another and that he still has his whole life ahead of him. He gives Thao the Silver Star awarded for his military service, and then goes in the evening to confront the gang himself at their house. Challenging them in a loud voice, which brings out all the neighbors, he tells Thao's cousin that he has no respect for anyone who would rape a member of his own family. When he prepares to light a cigarette, reaching into his jacket, the members of the gang think he is reaching for a gun; a fusillade of shots breaks out. Walt falls to the ground, dead. In his open, outstretched palm, no gun, but his Zippo lighter with the logo of the First Calvary with which he served. Sue finds Thao and releases him, and they arrive at the gang's apartment in the Gran Torino. By then, it's all over. The members of the gang are arrested, and a Hmong police officer tells the two that the neighbors have witnessed the whole confrontation and are willing to testify. In the final scene, when Walt's will is read before his family, he leaves his house to the church and the Gran Torino to Thao.

Both films show a personal transformation that comes about through friendship and compassion. Both show how those locked in their anger and loneliness can be opened to the Spirit. In *Dead Man Walking*, Sr. Helen breaks through Poncelet's isolation, showing him a concern that he may never have experienced in his difficult life. She wins his trust and accompanies him all the way to the end. In *Gran Torino*, the lovely young Sue charms Walt with her youth and goodness; more importantly, she brings him into the warmth of her Asian family where this lonely man is made to feel at home. In his relationship with Thao, he becomes the father and teacher he was not able to be to his own son. Both characters, Poncelet and Kowalski, are opened up to a goodness and love that is God. In their deaths, they die not alone but with a relationship, however dimly grasped, to the God who made them. And that God will bring them home. They have found salvation.

PART IV
CHURCH

18

MEETING JESUS

What was it that drew the first disciples to Jesus? How did their encounter with him affect them? Certainly Jesus was a charismatic figure; he must have been attractive, with a personal warmth and a gift for friendship. Those who became his disciples left behind home, family, and occupation; they gave up all and followed him. Their lives were changed.

CALL TO DISCIPLESHIP

Being a disciple of Jesus was different from being a disciple of the Pharisees, or even of the philosophers. The disciples' role was not to learn Jesus's teaching; they were to share in his ministry. When he sends them forth, he tells them, "As you go, proclaim the good news, 'The kingdom of heaven has come near.' Cure the sick, raise the dead, cleanse the lepers, cast out demons" (Matt 10:7–8). The disciples were to do what Jesus did. When we reflect on their experience, it seems clear that in their encounter with Jesus they came to experience in a very personal way God's love, God's saving power, and often a personal call to service. Let's consider the stories of a few of those figures we know from the New Testament.

Simon Peter, always first named among the Twelve, was clearly a significant figure in the historical ministry of Jesus and spokesman for the group. He was a fisherman, married, and a larger-than-life character. While spontaneously generous, Peter's self-knowledge didn't match his strong sense of self. When Jesus predicted that he would deny him, Peter declared himself ready to die with Jesus, yet swore he didn't know him when later that evening he was questioned by a mere servant girl. Yet Jesus saw something more in Peter; he was one of the first he called, promising him that he would be a "fisher of men." The various Petrine texts—singling out Peter as the rock on which Jesus would build his Church, the one who would strengthen his brethren, the pastor of the flock—all suggest some special role for Peter in the community.

Mary Magdalene, the woman who loved Jesus, was perhaps closest to him of anyone in the Gospels. While nothing in the New Testament suggests that Mary was a prostitute, her meeting with Jesus was transformative. Troubled by oppressive spirits, Luke tells us simply that seven demons had gone out of her after meeting Jesus (Luke 8:2). She became one of his disciples, following him to Calvary and witnessing his crucifixion. Going early Sunday morning to the tomb to anoint his body, she found it empty. According to a venerable tradition, Mary was the first to whom the risen Jesus manifested himself.

Saul of Tarsus, later Paul the Apostle, was a Pharisee and son of a Pharisee; he was educated at the feet of Gamaliel, celebrated in the Mishnah as one of Judaism's greatest teachers. Yet Saul was not at peace with himself; he was not free. Obsessed with his own righteousness, he describes himself as blameless with a righteousness based on his observance of the law (Phil 3:6), suggesting a rigidity of character, further evidenced by his persecution of other Jews who were followers of Jesus. His understanding of his Jewish heritage did not leave room for those with a different religious experience. Today, we would see him as a religious fanatic. But after his conversion, when, as he says, God was pleased to reveal his Son to me (Gal 1:15–16), he became the great Apostle of the Gentiles. Perhaps most significant of Paul's personal transformation is the fact that this once rigid Pharisee begins to write about the freedom enjoyed by the Christian (Gal 5:13; 1 Cor 6:12), once describing it in a lovely expression as the "freedom of the children of God" (Rom 8:21, NABRE).

Luke's story of Zacchaeus, the short-of-stature tax collector who climbed a tree in order to see Jesus passing through his town, may reflect someone known to the early Lukan community. The story is instructive. Zacchaeus makes a small effort to see Jesus, for which he is richly rewarded. Jesus greets him by name, inviting himself to stay at his house. The bystanders grumble, dismissing Zacchaeus as a sinner, but for Zacchaeus the encounter is a graced moment. He undergoes a conversion that includes making restitution, announcing, "Half of my possessions, Lord, I will give to the poor; and if I have defrauded any-one of anything, I will pay back four times as much" (Luke 19:8). Jesus tells him that salvation has come to his house.

The story of the Samaritan woman in the Gospel of John (4:1–39) is another example. This time, Jesus reaches out to an outsider, a woman and a Samaritan whom he met at a well in Samaria. As Jews of Judea and Galilee did not associate with Samaritans, his disciples, on their return, were "amazed" (v. 27, NABRE) that he was talking with the woman. Obviously, Jesus was not afraid to transgress social convention. But there is more; the woman has had five husbands, and the man she is living with at present is not her husband. The precise meaning here is not clear. For some, it means that the woman is a sinner. Others point out that a woman in that culture could not divorce her husband; she may have been the victim of abuse. In any case, Jesus draws her into a conversation, promis-ing her God's gift of living water, an Old Testament symbol of salvation. When the woman returns to her village, she points to the man she has encountered as the Messiah, and the villagers too come out to meet him.

LEARNING FROM THE STORIES

Each of these stories has certain common elements, suggesting something about what it means to encounter Jesus. For each of them, their encounter with him was a graced moment. First, each of the characters is in need of the grace of healing or forgiveness. Peter discovers his own weakness, is forgiven for his denial of his Lord, and is commissioned as pastor of those who follow Jesus, his "sheep" (John 21:15–17). The grace of this forgiveness became foundational to his religious experience. Mary Magdalene is set free from the spirits that oppressed her. We don't know what they were—addictions of various kinds, habits of sin, or psychological compulsions or fears. But she was liberated and became a different person. Paul was set free from his compelling need to justify himself before God, discovering grace not through observance of the law but through faith. His experience becomes central to his theology as Lutheran Christians have continued to emphasize. Zacchaeus makes restitution for those he may have defrauded; he becomes an honest man. The Samaritan woman is led from concern with her daily duties to hope in the coming Messiah. All are changed by their encounter with Jesus. Salvation has become real for each of them.

Second, most of them receive a call to discipleship or ecclesial service; they discover their vocations. Peter becomes the leader of the primitive community, helping make important decisions and holding the community together when tensions arise, as in the dispute over keeping kosher dietary regulations when Jewish and Gentile Christians come together for meals (Gal 2:11–12). He brings the good news to the Jews. The fisherman becomes an apostle. Mary Magdalene becomes a favorite disciple, faithful to the end and the first witness to the resurrection. After Jesus appears to her, he sends her to announce the news of the resurrection to the other disciples, the basis for the title *apostle* (John 20:17–18; cf. Mark 16:7). The later Church was to acknowledge her as the "apostle to the apostles." Paul, the former Pharisee, becomes the great Apostle to the Gentiles, founding churches whose names are still familiar to us today. Almost half of the New Testament is attributed to him, though some of the later books are written by his disciples. The woman of Samaria becomes a missionary disciple, bringing others to Jesus, and they come to recognize him as the Savior of the world.

Finally, each of the people we have considered enters into a personal relationship with Jesus, though we don't know anything further about Zacchaeus; his story in Luke's Gospel may reflect a later role in the early Christian community.

One story does not have a happy ending. It is the story of the rich man who met Jesus, asking what he must do to gain eternal life. Mark tells us that after reminding him of the commandments, all of which he had observed, Jesus, looking at him, loved him and said, "You lack one thing; go, sell what you own, and give the money to the poor, and you will have treasure in heaven; then come, follow me." But the man was not free enough to accept the invitation. Mark tells us that "he was shocked and went away grieving, for he had many possessions" (Mark 10:17–22). The tragedy here is that this man, loved by Jesus, was not able to respond to a very personal call to discipleship.

Who knows what gifts he might have brought to the early Church, had he welcomed the invitation. Obviously a good man, leading a moral life, and with a certain generosity of spirit, he was lacking in spiritual freedom. Did he have talents that he was not yet aware of? Could he have been another Paul, a missionary apostle, helping to spread the good news, founding churches? Might he have become another evangelist, leaving for posterity letters on the Christian life or even a gospel? Did Jesus see a future for him beyond his ability to imagine? Whatever that future might have been, it is clear that he gave up an invitation for a personal relationship with Jesus, one that might have developed into an intimate friendship.

What can we learn from these stories? In each case, the persons in question discover something about themselves, becoming more aware of their need for healing or forgiveness. Second, those who open themselves to Jesus experience God's transforming grace in some personal way. Finally, each becomes an import figure in the Jesus story or the life of the early Church. Those who experience God's love and salvation in their encounter with Jesus become disciples, missionaries, evangelists, or apostles. They want to bring the good news to others.

The people we have been considering were changed by their meeting with Jesus. And so should we be. Some years ago, when I was teaching in China, I knew a group of young people in an RCIA program preparing for baptism. Before the Easter Vigil liturgy, the sister in charge of preparing the candidates asked each how their own lives would change with baptism. One young man, very bright but perhaps less mature, said he didn't think his life would really change. The sister decided that he was not ready, and asked him to delay his baptism. A priest friend of the young man interceded with the bishop on his behalf, but the bishop backed the nun.

MISSIONARY DISCIPLES TODAY

I've often wondered why so many Catholics today, especially younger ones, seem unable or unwilling to share their faith with others. They are not very Evangelical. They consider their faith a private matter, which is how our American culture thinks religion should remain. Some find it difficult to explain Catholic teachings and traditions to others. Others think, mistakenly, that being "Evangelical" is Protestant. Maybe they are uncomfortable with Evangelical proselytizing, or with being confronted by them, asking them if they have been saved. Some are still negotiating their own relationship with the Church. They have their own struggles with those teachings that seem counterintuitive to them, with authority that often seems unresponsive to the needs of God's people today, and with the failures of the Church. They find the Church unsympathetic to the concerns of women, gays, and lesbians, or to the divorced and remarried. Some have not forgotten the scandal of sexual abuse by clergy.

Others, like the rich man in the Gospel of Mark, may find that their possessions or "lifestyle" gets in the way. In the "First Principle and Foundation," at the beginning of the *Spiritual Exercises*, St. Ignatius says that we should be "detached" or "indifferent" to all created things (*indiferentes á todas las cosas criadas*) in order to choose those things that will lead us to the end for which we were created. In more contemporary language, he is speaking of a spiritual freedom, the exact opposite of an attachment to things.

We need to ask ourselves, are we free enough to hear God's call? Do we have enough inner silence to hear the quiet voice of God, not dramatic, often just "a sound of sheer silence" (1 Kgs 19:12). Do we even ask what plans our God might have for us? Or are we like the man in the gospel story, hearing but unable to respond to the invitation of Jesus? Sometimes we are afraid to let the Lord get too close to us. The evil spirit starts surfacing objections. We fear that God might make some demand of us; that we will become ill, have to suffer, or be called upon to make some great sacrifice. So we keep our distance.

And yet the young Catholics I meet are often very generous. This is especially true of our students. Many give hours to community outreach and service; others volunteer for postgraduate service programs. The same is true of our graduate students. I am always impressed with those that come to us to pursue further studies in theology. They want to serve the Church. They work as high school teachers, campus ministers, spiritual directors, pastoral associates in parishes, or go on to doctoral studies in theology. They struggle to present the Church and its teaching in a positive light to their own students, to find some way to reach them, to tune in to their wave length. What do these grad students want of the Church? They want good preaching, vibrant liturgies, and compassionate ministers.

Some years ago, I was at the Archdiocese of Los Angeles Religious Education Congress, the largest in the world with some forty thousand in attendance, when I ran into a former student. She was a young Hispanic woman, a girl then, who in my freshmen class rarely spoke; she practically disappeared. But her quizzes and papers were outstanding, drawing my attention to her. I asked her if she ever thought of majoring in theology, and she acknowledged that she "kind of liked theology." Later she declared a major, but I lost track of her, only to encounter her over fifteen years later at the Congress. She was now a self-assured young woman, teaching religion in a Catholic high school and loving it. This was another graced moment, leading me to marvel at God's mysterious ways.

The desire to touch others is very much in harmony with Pope Francis's vision of the Church, for his favorite image of a Christian is that of a missionary disciple. In his apostolic exhortation *Evangelii gaudium*, the Joy of the Gospel, he calls for a missionary transformation of the Church. A Church sure in the knowledge that the Lord has loved us first is empowered to take the initiative; it goes out to others, seeks those who have fallen away, stands at the crossroads, and welcomes the outcasts. It seeks always to show mercy as we have experienced God's mercy, "touching the suffering flesh of Christ in others" (no. 24).

Basic to the pope's thought is that those who have truly encountered Jesus and accepted his offer of salvation have been filled with the joy of the gospel, and it is the nature of goodness always to spread, as the scholastics taught (*bonum est sui diffusium*). Thus, Francis dreams of a "missionary option," a missionary impulse capable of transforming everything, so that the Church's customs, ways of doing things, times and schedules, language and structures, can be suitably channeled for the evangelization of today's world rather than for her own self-preservation (no. 27). He says, "In virtue of their baptism, all the members of the People of God have become missionary disciples (cf. *Mt* 28:19). All the baptized, whatever their position in the Church or their level of instruction in the faith, are agents of evangelization, and it would be insufficient to envisage a plan of evangelization to be carried out by professionals while the rest of the faithful would simply be passive recipients" (EG 120).

Will the pope's dream of a missionary Church become a reality? Too many find the concept difficult. They are more accustomed to what some have described as a "service station" model of Church, where the faithful come to receive their sacraments and request their Masses for the dead. But a change is already underway with the explosion of lay ministries that followed the Second Vatican Council. Jesus did not come to create customers. He came to call men and women to discipleship, to a share in his ministry.

19

THE WORD

Words are always important. They can comfort, heal, or establish a relationship. We reach out to others with our words, express our feelings, welcome a friend, or forgive someone who has hurt us. When someone says, "I love you," our world is brightened and takes on color; we see ourselves in a new way. We return over and over to that moment, to savor it again.

But words can also wound, tear, or alienate. How often has a thoughtless remark of a friend or acquaintance poisoned a relationship? We cannot get beyond it, and as a result, we cherish resentment and feel awkward in that person's presence. We can easily damage or destroy another person's reputation by repeating stories that tear them down, rather than build them up. Children especially can be careless with words, name-calling, teasing the vulnerable, and ridiculing another.

The ancient Israelites had a powerful sense of the word. Once spoken, a blessing or a curse, the word could not be recalled. Remember Isaac, who tricked his father into giving him the blessing intended for his hirsute older brother by covering his hands and neck with the skin of a goat (Gen 27:16). Covenants were agreements, verbal or written, between two parties or between city-states, spelling out rights and obligations; they provided a model for expressing God's relationship with the people, Israel.

THE WORD OF GOD

Far more powerful than human words was the word of God! Unlike the creation myths of their neighbors, in which, after a cosmic struggle, the Earth was fashioned from the dead body of Tiamat, the monster goddess of chaos, who represented the formless but relentlessly hostile sea, the God of Israel calls the heavens and earth into being by the sheer power of the divine word (Gen 1:1—2:4a). God spoke and the world and all within it was made. The prophets were empowered with the word of God, calling God's people to conversion, assuring them of God's love or threatening them with his judgment. Isaiah sees the word going forth from the mouth of God to accomplish the divine will, achieving the end that God intended (Isa 55:11).

Thus *word* in Hebrew (*dabar*) was dynamic, an extension of the power and personality of the speaker. Once spoken, it went forth to accomplish its purpose. It was a soteriological principle. In Greek, *word* (*logos*) was a cosmological principle, a principle of meaning or organization. It could be translated as either "word" or "reason." *Logos* gave form to the cosmos and meaning to the sounds of the human voice.

In the Prologue of the Fourth Gospel, the Greek, *logos*, reflects both the Hebrew and Greek understanding of *word*; it is both soteriological and cosmological. The Word was divine, personal, with God from the beginning, active in creation: "All things came into being through him, and without him not one thing came into being" (John 1:3). And it was coming into the world to work God's salvation: "But to all who received him, who believed in his name, he gave power to become children of God" (John 1:12). "And the Word became flesh and lived among us, and we have seen his glory, the glory as of a father's only son, full of grace and truth" (John 1:14).

Behind the imagery of the Prologue is the idea of God, the source of all being, speaking from eternity into time the Divine Word, the image of the Divine Mystery as both reason and love, the Word that becomes flesh in the person of Jesus of Nazareth. Pope Benedict XVI unites these two metaphors for the Divine Mystery, the philosophical and the interpersonal, in his encyclical *Deus caritas est*: "God is the absolute and ultimate source of all being; but this universal principle of creation—the *Logos*, primordial reason—is at the same time a lover with all the passion of a true love" (no. 10).

Already in the Old Testament, the word became text, as Israel committed its traditions to writing. Second Kings 23 portrays King Josiah (ca. 640–609 BC) initiating a reform based on scrolls found in the temple containing the Law of Deuteronomy. The Book of Nehemiah, set during the Exile in Babylon, shows Ezra reading from "the Law" to a large gathering of people (Neh 8:1–3). In fifth century Judah after the return from exile, the priestly editors wove together earlier traditions, some in written form, into the Pentateuch or Torah (the Law). Thus, when St. Paul talks about the "Scriptures," he is referring to the sacred writings of the Jewish people, while his own letters would constitute almost a third of what would be called the "New Testament."

The writings of the Church fathers were nourished by both testaments. Jerome's late-fourth-century Vulgate, a Latin translation of the Hebrew and Greek Scriptures, became the standard Bible for the Western Church, but by the Middle Ages, most Christians could no longer read Latin. Some vernacular translations existed, but it was really the Reformers who, in holding up the Bible against the Church, returned the Bible to a privileged place in Christian life, at least for Protestants. Luther's German Bible (1534) contributed to the development of the modern German language, while the King James Bible (1611) surpassed the influence even of Shakespeare in the development of modern English.

Unfortunately, post-Reformation Catholicism tended to treat the Bible as a Protestant book. Catholic children in parochial schools learned the biblical stories from richly illustrated textbooks but did not read the Bible itself. Too often the stereotype was true: Protestantism was a Church of the word; Catholicism of the sacraments. In my early days as a Jesuit novice, we never had a sermon or homily at Mass, not even on Sundays. Even today, many Protestants have a better biblical knowledge than those Catholics whose lives are not nourished by Sacred Scripture.

DEI VERBUM

But that has largely changed. One of the most significant reforms of the Second Vatican Council was its restoring the Bible to its proper place in the life of the Church. Stressing that "ignorance of the Scriptures is ignorance of Christ" (no. 25), the Dogmatic Constitution on Divine Revelation, *Dei Verbum*, played a major role in placing the word of God at the center of Christian life, liturgy, and theology. The constitution taught that the "Church has always venerated the divine Scriptures just as she venerates the body of the Lord" (no. 21)—a very strong statement, placing reverence for the word on a par with reverence for the Eucharist. It mandated that all the faithful should have easy access to Sacred Scripture in translations prepared with the help of other Christians; it taught that the study of Scripture is the soul of sacred theology just as it must inform pastoral preaching, catechetics, and all Christian instruction, "in which the liturgical homily must hold the foremost place" (no. 24). So every liturgy should have at least a brief homily.

The Council's revision of the lectionary also helped recenter Catholic worship on the word of God. A three-year Sunday and a two-year weekday cycle seeks to cover as much of the Bible as possible. It can be argued that with such a lectionary, Catholics become familiar in their worship with much more of the Bible than those Protestant communities that don't have a lectionary and are dependent on the weekly choice of the preacher. I was once asked to preside at a local Congregational Church when the pastor was on vacation. When I inquired what the readings were, he told me, "Whatever you want." Of course many of the more liturgical Protestant churches use a lectionary, sometimes even the Catholic one, which means that many Christians from different traditions are reflecting on the same readings each Sunday.

There are many ways to integrate Scripture into daily prayer. Many Christians have rediscovered the divine office or breviary, long prayed by monks in choir and priests in private. Revised by the Council, the office or "Liturgy of the Hours" consists basically of Morning

Prayer, Evening Prayer, an Office of Readings, and Compline. Most hours consist of an introductory hymn, three psalms and a canticle, a brief Scripture reading, and some prayers of petition. Abbreviated versions of the Liturgy of the Hours appear in popular mini-missalettes such as *Magnificat* (The Catholic Company), *Living with Christ* (Novalis), or *Give Us This Day* (Liturgical Press).

Some are never without their Bibles. Others like to start the day by reading and contemplating the daily readings from one of these missalettes, or just the gospel of the day. Not just our days, but our lives should be illumined by the word of God. God continues to speak to us through the words of Sacred Scripture. I remember, when trying to make up my mind about entering the religious life, being powerfully struck one morning at daily Mass by the *Introit*, the entrance antiphon for the liturgy, then still in Latin. What I heard was a verse from the Last Discourse in the Gospel of John: "You did not choose me but I chose you. And I appointed you to go and bear fruit, fruit that will last" (John 15:16). I heard those words as addressed to me personally; it was a message from the Lord.

Jesus warns us in the Gospels that we have to prepare good soil to receive the word. Sometimes, it falls on the path where it is trodden underfoot and cannot grow. Too often, it falls on rocky ground, but without roots, it withers away in times of trial. For others, it falls among the thorns, the thorns of worldly anxieties, the lure of riches, and desires for earthly pleasures that choke it.

In his *Spiritual Exercises*, Ignatius of Loyola encourages an imaginative contemplative of the gospel "mysteries" or stories. He invites the retreatant to place him or herself into the gospel scene, for example, at the Nativity, forming a mental image of the scene, imagining the road from Nazareth to Bethlehem, whether level or winding over hills and through valleys, seeing the cave at Nazareth and him or herself ministering to the holy family, perhaps even holding the infant Jesus. Entering into the mystery in this way can bring it alive in our imagination; we become more familiar with the characters, sometimes notice things we otherwise have missed, or enter into a dialogue with the characters.

Through this kind of contemplation, the gospel stories become a part of us. Often their human dimensions awaken something in our own humanity, and heart begins to speak to heart. We deepen a relationship with the God who has first loved us.

The *Spiritual Exercises* are only one way of focusing on the word of God. But whether through the *Exercises*, using the gospel text, a daily missalette, a family Bible occupying an honored place in one's home, a daily verse from Scripture reflected on during the day, God's word should nourish our imaginations and our lives. For God continues to speak to each of us through Scripture.

20

EUCHARIST

Food is an important symbol in the Bible. It is necessary for life; without it we perish. But there is also a social meaning to food; a meal brings people together in communion and helps them create community. It can be a kind of sacrament. We decorate the table with a pretty cloth and linen napkins, bring it to life with flowers, and light candles to create an atmosphere of warmth and hospitality. Food can help break down cultural barriers in a parish, bringing people together with food from different traditions. At first it may seem strange: What is this? What do you call it? Can I try it? Good, very good. Often sharing food across cultural boundaries leads to conversation, greater understanding, and communion.

BREAD FROM HEAVEN

In the Bible, God both gathers and nourishes his people. The Pasch or Passover Supper, a ritual meal celebrated with story and symbol, recalls the liberation of the children of Israel from slavery in Egypt, making them a people. During their wandering in the desert, God fed them with manna, "bread from heaven," and gave them water from the rock to drink. When they continued to grumble against him, he sent quail into their camp so they might eat and have their fill of meat.

The biblical tradition recognizes as well the deeper hungers of God's people, hungers not always recognized. Sometimes they emerge into consciousness. Isaiah recognized this implicitly. In trying to image God's salvation, he used the image of a great eschatological feast to satisfy Israel's hunger, the hungers of the human spirit.

> On this mountain the LORD of hosts will make for all
> peoples
> a feast of rich food, a feast of well-aged wines,
> of rich food filled with marrow, of well-aged wines
> strained clear.
>
> (Isa 25:6)

Our hunger for food and drink can symbolize our deeper appetites, our desires for life, for immortality, for God. In his vision, Isaiah saw God's salvation being revealed to all people from this mountain in the heavenly Jerusalem. "Then the Lord GOD will wipe away the tears from all faces" (Isa 25:8).

Jesus appropriated this image, using it to foreshadow the banquet when many will come from the east and the west to recline with Abraham, Isaac, and Joseph in the kingdom of heaven (Matt 8:10–12; cf. Luke 13:26–30). In his preaching, the image also became at times the great wedding feast, though it demanded that one have a wedding garment (Matt 22:1–14; cf. Luke 14:15–24). Meals played an important role in the ministry of Jesus. He shared meals with his disciples and religious leaders like Simon the Pharisee (Luke 7:36–50) and provided a bountiful meal of bread and fish for the multitudes that followed him. His inclusive table fellowship with the religiously marginal, symbolizing that no one was excluded from God's reign, drew constant criticism; they charged, this man eats with tax collectors and sinners (Matt 9:11; 11:19).

THE EUCHARIST OF JESUS

At his last meal with the Twelve, the Paschal Supper according to the Synoptics, Jesus transformed the supper into a memorial of his offering of his life for others, "for the many" or "for all," depending on the translation. He identified the bread and wine of the table with his body broken and blood poured out. Not only does he nourish his own out of his own substance, but his blood becomes the sign of a new covenant between God and God's people. Faithful to the command to repeat Paul and Luke's version of the "institution narrative," the Church has to the present day continued to gather around the table to break bread and share the cup in memory of Jesus. Paul calls this the "Lord's supper" (1 Cor 11:20), but from the late first or early second century, Christians were calling it the Eucharist (*Didache*, Ignatius of Antioch), from the great prayer of "thanksgiving" (*eucharistein*) prayed by the presider. Today, Christians refer to the sacrament as the Mass, the Divine Liturgy, the Lord's Supper, holy communion, or the breaking of the bread.

The early Christians gathered in the catacombs of Rome to celebrate the Eucharist at tombs of the martyrs. The apologist Justin Martyr (d. 165) left a description of an early Eucharist that was virtually the same as it is today, though apparently the prayer of thanksgiving was prayed spontaneously. The Eucharist was celebrated on Sunday, "the Lord's day" (Rev 1:10) or first day of the week, the day on which God created the world as well as the day on which Jesus rose from the dead. Justin refers to a financial offering for the poor and says that the deacons helped with the distribution of the bread and wine, and would bring the sacrament to those unable to be present. Early churches were generally oriented toward the east, so that the congregation and presider might greet Christ when he came again, like the sun, from the east. In a real sense, the Eucharist brings Isaiah's vision of the eschatological banquet into time; in receiving Christ's body and blood, we become one with Jesus and so with God who is our salvation and our destiny.

The whole sixth chapter of John's Gospel is a meditation on Jesus as the living bread come down from heaven. Beginning with the miracle of the loaves, itself a eucharistic symbol of an eschatological fullness with twelve wicker baskets of leftover fragments, it moves through Jesus's description of himself as the bread come down from heaven, the bread that gives life to the world, to finally an explicitly eucharistic command to eat his flesh and drink his blood, the food and drink of union with him now and of our sharing in his resurrection on the last day.

PAST, PRESENT, AND FUTURE

Thus, the Eucharist is a polyvalent symbol, bringing together past, present, and future. This is beautifully expressed in the antiphon *O Sacrum Convivium* composed by Thomas Aquinas for the Feast of Corpus Christi:

> O sacred banquet!
> in which Christ is received,
> the memory of his Passion is renewed,
> the mind is filled with grace,
> and a pledge of future glory is given to us.
> Alleluia.

In recalling Jesus's offering of his life, ministry, and death for us, "for the forgiveness of sins," his sacrifice becomes present through narrative and ritual. In this way, the Eucharist takes on a sacrificial dimension. For St. Augustine, every work that affects our union with God is a true sacrifice. Catholics were once accustomed to speak of the Eucharist as the "Holy Sacrifice of the Mass." More importantly than the name is joining our sacrifices to his, laying them on the altar with our gifts, offering our own lives to the God who so loves us. This is an expression of the baptismal priesthood, enabling us to enter into the paschal mystery of Jesus's passage from death to life.

In the Eucharist, Jesus is both host and guest. He invites us to his supper and gives us himself, his body and blood. We encounter him as guest of honor and are joined in intimate union with him who meets us in sacramental signs. This is the present dimension of the sacrament. We are united with Christ and he is united with us. How often I have sensed this in ministering the bread or the cup at Mass. You see it in the eyes and on the faces of the people coming to communion. Sometimes it is joy, evident in moist eyes and the tears that sometimes flow. Sometimes it is awe before the mystery, reflected in bodily reverence. Sometimes it is hope in the midst of suffering or pain. Often it is love. Ronald Rolheiser sees the union of sexual intercourse as a fitting metaphor for the Eucharist:

> In the Eucharist, Christ touches us, intimately, physically, sensually, carnally. Eucharist is physical, not spiritual; its embrace real, as physical as the incarnation itself. In this way, Eucharist is more radical than is the Word. Indeed the relationship of the Word to the Eucharist is most accurately and profitably understood within the metaphor of physical embrace and sexual intercourse (and this may be more than metaphor). The Word is sacramental, but it is less physical than the Eucharist. The communion it creates is less physical than is Eucharistic union. In a manner of speaking, the Word is a preparation for, a readying for, making love. Its role is to prepare us for Eucharistic communion. The Eucharist is the touch, the physical coming together, the embrace, the consummation, the intercourse.[1]

The Eucharist also unites us in all our difference and disunity as Christ's Body. No one has said that more beautifully than St. Paul, in what may be his most important insight into Church. He writes, "The cup of blessing that we bless, is it not a sharing (*koinōnia*) in the blood of Christ? The bread that we break, is it not a sharing in the body of Christ? Because there is one bread, we who are many are one body, for we all partake of the one bread" (1 Cor 10:16–17). The Greek word *koinōnia* means "a sharing or participation" in something else, thus communion or sometimes fellowship. We have a communion or sharing in Christ's body and blood, and so are made one with him and with all those joined in this holy communion.

At the same time, we are joined in communion with all those who have gone before us, those we sometimes refer to as the "Church triumphant" living now in Christ—our parents and departed members of our families and friends, as well as the saints throughout the ages. The Catholic practice of invoking Mary and the saints is rooted in this doctrine of the "communion of saints" that we confess in the Apostles' Creed. There is evidence of Christians asking the intercession of Mary as early as the third century (c. 250). Augustine, preaching on the feasts of the martyrs, conveyed the idea of one community of those on earth and the martyrs in heaven who prayed for those still on the way. When we are together for the Eucharist, heaven is not far away. John Nava's wonderful tapestry bringing to life the walls of the Cathedral of our Lady of the Angels in Los Angeles is a celebration of the communion of saints, a great procession of the faithful whether canonized officially or by the devotion of the faithful.

Sometimes in receiving the Eucharist I think of all those saints whose stories and example have touched me personally, my own communion of saints. My parents first of all who gave me life and the faith; Ignatius of Loyola, Francis Xavier, Peter Faber, and the other first Jesuits who formed the company in which I have long lived; Francis of Assisi, Thomas Aquinas, Teresa of Avila, and Karl Rahner, theologians and mystics whose witness lives on in the Church; Alfred Delp, Dietrich Bonhoeffer, Edith Stein, and Etty Hillesum, the first two executed shortly before the end of the Second World War for their resistance to Nazi tyranny, the last two, both Jews, one of whom became a Catholic and a Carmelite nun, who were murdered at Auschwitz; Thomas Merton, Oscar Romero and the four Church women murdered in El Salvador in 1980; Ignacio Ellacuría and his brother Jesuits assassinated in their residence almost ten years later; Mother Teresa and Pope John XXIII.

These are my saints; they have touched my life and given me courage or hope. I know I am united with them in the sacrament of the altar; we are in communion, truly one in Christ.

Finally, the Eucharist looks to the future. It is an anticipation of our union with God in the kingdom when we are no longer dependent on signs, seeing indistinctly as in a mirror, but then we will see God face-to-face and "then I will know fully, even as I have been fully known" (cf. 1 Cor 13:12). Then God will dwell with us and we will dwell with God. Echoing the promise of Isaiah, the author of the Book of Revelation says,

> God himself will be with them;
> he will wipe every tear from their eyes.
> Death will be no more;
> mourning and crying and pain will be no more,
> for the first things have passed away.
>
> (Rev 21:3–4)

The Eucharist is indeed the food of everlasting life.

21

BODY OF CHRIST

Among the many metaphors for Church in the New Testament, three are especially important: people of God, Body of Christ, and temple of the Spirit. While all three are Pauline, people of God is presumed throughout the New Testament. It emphasizes the continuity of the Church with God's people of the first covenant, Israel, a point of particular importance for Paul, the former Pharisee. Paul also sees the Church as a community animated by the Holy Spirit, thus we are God's coworkers, God's field, God's building or temple (cf. 1 Cor 3:9, 16); he calls the Church a temple sacred in the Lord and the dwelling place of God in the Spirit (cf. Eph 2:21–22). The Church is thus a charismatic community, animated by the Spirit, a point often lost in Catholicism's at times overemphasis on the Church's hierarchical structure. But Paul's most powerful metaphor is Body of Christ.

THE BODY OF CHRIST

In Hellenistic culture, *body* was used to characterize anything constituted by parts, whether civic, cosmological, or rhetorical. Paul uses *body* as early as his First Letter to the Corinthians to speak of the Christian assembly or Church as one Body, made one in receiving the cup of blessings and the bread broken in the Eucharist (1 Cor 10:16–17), just as its members have been united by baptism (1 Cor 12:13). Indeed, it is in 1 Corinthians 12 that Paul develops his image of the Church as the one Body of Christ. Comparing it to the human body, he sees the Church as a body with different members, equipped with various gifts and ministries (cf. Rom 12:3–8), and united in the one Spirit. Thus the Church is constituted by God's Spirit, mediated by baptism and Eucharist; it has a sacramental foundation.

Paul's thought is echoed in a beautiful verse in a chapter from the *Didache* or *Teaching of the Twelve Apostles*, an instruction on baptism, Eucharist, and Christian living dating from the mid- to late-first century: The unknown author prays, "Even as this broken bread was scattered over the hills, and was gathered together and became one, so let Thy Church be gathered together from the ends of the earth into Thy kingdom; for Thine is the glory and the power through Jesus Christ forever."

THE TRUE BODY

In the history of the Church, the phrase *mystical body* (*corpus mysticum*) originally referred to the sacramental or eucharistic body of Christ. The phrase *Body of Christ* or *true Body of Christ* (*verum corpus*) referred to the Church, in the Pauline sense. But a controversy in the eleventh century with Berengar, a theologian and head of the school of St. Martin at Tours, over Christ's eucharistic presence led to a reversal of this traditional language. Berengar seems to have taught that Christ was present in the Eucharist only as *sign*, rather than that the bread was identical with his body. In response to what seemed to many an overly symbolic approach, Berengar was forced in 1059 to make a rather literal confession of faith, affirming that after the consecration, the bread becomes the true body of the Lord "broken by the hands of the priest and crushed by the teeth of the faithful." Martin Luther later used similar language. The Fourth Lateran Council (1215) used the term *transubstantiation* to affirm that while the appearances of the bread and wine remained the same, the substance of both really changed, introducing the term that has become traditional for many Catholics today.

The controversy with Berengar contributed to an unfortunate shift in meaning; the *verum corpus* or true body became the eucharistic species, while the Church became the mystical Body, the term for the Church used by Pope Pius XII in his 1943 encyclical, *Mystici Corporis Christi*. The result of this shift was the development of an overly individualistic eucharistic piety.[1] Lost was the relationship between eucharistic participation and Church, uniting the members into the one body of Christ, so evident in Paul (cf. 1 Cor 10:16–17). This came home to me powerfully one Sunday. As the priest raised the large host at the consecration, I was suddenly struck with the realization that here was the risen Jesus present in the midst of his people. We were not alone, not just a crowd assembled, but Jesus was here, gathering us into his body, making us Church. In a homily preached on January 1, 2015, Pope Francis proclaimed, "Our faith is not an abstract doctrine or philosophy, but a vital and full relationship with a person: Jesus Christ, the only-begotten Son of God who became man, was put to death, rose from the dead to save us, and is now living in our midst. Where can we encounter him? We encounter him in the Church, in our hierarchical, Holy Mother Church."[2]

MAKING JESUS PRESENT

To say that the Church is the Body of Christ is to affirm that the risen Jesus becomes visible and carries on his ministry through this local Christian community as well as through the Church spread throughout the world. The risen Jesus lives in God's eternal present; he is no longer bound by the limitations of space and time. He is fully with God, and at the same time, he is present in his disciples, those baptized in his Spirit. The Church is not a big, abstract institution; it is faces, bodies, and people. The Church and Christ are inseparable; it is the sacrament of the risen Christ, making him present in sign and work. Christ is present in the Word proclaimed (kerygma), the ministry of the Church (*diakonia*), in its communion or fellowship (*koinonia*), and its worship (*liturgia*). As Terrence Tilley says in reference to the Church, "What in the world could Christ do without his body?"[3]

We are not just our bodies, but embodied spirits. Spirit animates our bodies and becomes visible in our bodily gaze, gestures, and expressions, as anyone sensitive to "body language" knows so well. Much, positive or negative, is disclosed by this language of the body. In moments of encounter, we notice how someone moves forward to greet us or draws back, retreating out of reach. Our eyes reveal much in a glance or gaze; our pupils open or contract, become warm or harden. As the saying goes, "The eyes are the windows of the soul." A handshake or embrace, arms crossed defensively or open in welcome, a caress or a kiss—these gestures communicate so much, unveiling the spirit within. The physical joining of two bodies can be a sign of love and self-gift, or of a violent using of the other. So often our actions speak louder than our words.

So it is with Church, Christ's Body. St. Theresa of Avila expressed this beautifully in a poem:

> Christ has no body but yours,
> No hands, no feet on earth but yours,
> Yours are the eyes with which he looks
> Compassion on this world,
> Yours are the feet with which he walks to do good,
> Yours are the hands, with which he blesses all the world.
> Yours are the hands, yours are the feet,
> Yours are the eyes, you are his body.
> Christ has no body now but yours,
> No hands, no feet on earth but yours,
> Yours are the eyes with which he looks
> compassion on this world.
> Christ has no body now on earth but yours.

A consciousness of ourselves as Christ's Body can ennoble our ministry, our efforts to live lives of service. Our good works and acts of charity take on new meaning. Christ reaches out to others through us; we bring them his healing and compassion; we can image God's mercy. We help others to come to know him. But the opposite is also true; a thoughtless word or gesture can alienate others. We can contribute to the disengagement or unbelief so widespread today. We can be points of light or increase the darkness. Think of the thousands damaged, estranged from the Church due to harsh words from those who are Church ministers, and especially those young people who were the victims of sexual abuse at the hands of clergy. What a tragedy!

Most Catholics of a certain generation grew up with a reverence for the eucharistic body of Christ. Prior to the Second Vatican Council, only the priest could touch the Blessed Sacrament, or even the sacred vessels of the altar: the paten, chalice, or ciboria. Some priests would scrupulously rinse and polish the chalice endlessly, to make sure no particle of bread remained. If he dropped a host, he would cover the spot on the floor with a purificator, and return after the Mass to wash the spot clean of any trace of the host.

After the Council, laymen and women began to take on the ministry of extraordinary ministers of the Eucharist. Though some Catholics were uncomfortable at first receiving the Eucharist from a layperson, they came to recognize that the hands of those baptized and sharing in the priesthood of Christ were as holy as any gold vessel on the altar. This should not diminish any reverence we have for the eucharistic bread.

Dorothy Day, who with Peter Maurin founded the Catholic Worker movement, had a deeply eucharistic faith. At the end of her famous autobiography, she wrote, "We cannot love God unless we love each other, and to love we must know each other. We know Him in the breaking of bread, and we know each other in the breaking of bread, and we are not alone any more."[4] Once a famous priest involved in the anti-war movement celebrated a simple Eucharist at the Catholic Worker community in New York, using a loaf of French bread and a cup of wine at a table where so many had been fed. After the liturgy, as community members gathered around the priest, someone noticed that Dorothy was missing. They found her on her knees on the floor, gathering up the pieces of bread that had fallen during the communion. Her reverence for the eucharistic fragments were of a piece with her reverence for the poor, gathered by the ministry of the Catholic Worker community; Christ is present in both.

We should have the same reverence for the members of Christ's Body, the Church; we are members of one another, united in the Body of Christ and the one Spirit. In some monastic communities, the monks, while processing into the sanctuary for the liturgy, pause and bow, first to the tabernacle and then to each other. Christ is present in both.

Unfortunately, the Body of Christ in history has been wounded, its unity broken; the Church of Christ is divided into different communities and churches, diminishing its witness of unity and communion. The history of the Church and the churches is a sorry story of mutual excommunications, religious wars, alienation, and hostility. But that began to change in the early twentieth century with the beginning of the ecumenical movement for Christian unity. While initially disinterested, the Catholic Church eventually embraced ecumenism at the Second Vatican Council, but that is a story for later.

22

Holy Families

I used to wonder why the Feast of the Holy Family occurred right after Christmas; it always seemed rather secondary to the mystery being celebrated. But as I've grown older, I've come to see how appropriate its place in the liturgical calendar actually is. For if we take the central meaning of the incarnation seriously, that in Jesus, God became man—took on flesh—then it was precisely in his family that the boy Jesus was shaped into the man he became.

His life hidden in Nazareth is a good subject for contemplation. As the Gospels tell us, it was in his home at Nazareth, subject to his parents, that Jesus advanced in wisdom and age and favor before God and man (see Luke 2:52). Certainly, Jesus learned about Yahweh God at an early age, instructed by his parents, who shared the stories of their tradition with their beloved child. From them he learned to take part in the religious life of his people.

His mother, Mary, would have wiped away the tears of his childhood, comforting him, teaching him the tender care he later showed for others. His foster father, Joseph, in his quiet way, showed him how to be a person of integrity, a responsible young man and adult. From him Jesus learned his trade; later he was known simply as "the carpenter" (Mark 6:3). His preaching shows a familiarity with the Scriptures; most probably he was literate. From the village elders he learned the stories of the prophets, with their hope of a future intervention of God in the life of the people. On the Sabbath, he joined the prayer in the synagogue (Luke 4:16). He must also have been familiar with the Wisdom tradition, with its story of the just man who puts himself in God's hand, seeing himself as a child of God and calling God his "Father" (Wis 2:12–20). The Wisdom tradition is reflected in his preaching.

FAMILY LIFE TODAY

But family life today in our western countries is in trouble. In an age of overexposure on social networks, relationships are often superficial. Commitment is difficult. As of 2012, it was estimated probable that 40 to 50 percent of marriages would end in divorce. The number of petitions for annulments in the United States has dropped from a high of 72,308 in 1990 to 18,558 in 2014, while between 1970 and 2014 the number of Catholic marriages dropped from 420,000 to 154,000, suggesting that fewer Catholics are marrying in the church or seeking to take advantage of the annulment process.[1] Many don't bother with marriage, sacramental or civil. An increasing number of Catholics forego both institution and the sacrament. At the same time, a 2011 study at the University of Iowa found that loss of virginity before age eighteen correlated with a greater occurrence of divorce in the first ten years of marriage. Our culture is one of broken relationships and shattered lives.

In the west, birthrates per one thousand persons continue to fall. According to statistics gathered by the World Bank, most African countries have between thirty-five to forty-nine births per one thousand people, while in Western Europe, the average is about ten, with Germany the lowest at eight. On a recent stay in Germany, I saw few German women with babies, while those pushing baby carriages, often with two small children, were almost always Muslim. The United States has fourteen births per one thousand, the United Kingdom thirteen, and France thirteen. It is difficult to argue that the sexual revolution has been all that liberating. As Thomas Reese has suggested, "With the changes in sexual attitudes have come increases in pornography, extramarital sex, date rape, sexual activity among children, illegitimacy, abortion, adultery, divorce and sexually transmitted diseases, to say nothing of broken hearts."[2]

From the earliest days of the Church, Christian families stood out from the surrounding culture. The second-century Epistle to Diognetus said of Christians, "Like others, they marry and have children, but they do not expose them. They share their meals, but not their wives."[3] From the beginning, children were valued; abortion and the exposing of newborn, widely practiced in the Roman Empire, was condemned. The late-first-century document, *Didache*, says, "You shall not murder a child by abortion nor kill that which is born."[4] The same sentence appears in the noncanonical Letter of Barnabas, written probably between 70 and 130.

Marriage is never easy. My own experience is at best secondhand, but as I have watched friends, former students, and members of my family mature into marriage, become parents, struggle with all that is necessary to make a marriage a success, I appreciate how hard they have to work and the sacrifices that are involved. And there are many single-parent families where a father or mother makes heroic sacrifices for the good of their children.

THE SCHOOL OF LOVE

Marriage is the great school of love. It is where we discover ourselves as precious to another and learn to be loving ourselves; we also discover much about the love of God. In a Christmas address to the Roman Curia shortly before he announced his retirement, Pope Benedict spoke of the difficulty of making commitments today, suggesting that for many a commitment was seen as a violation of human freedom or not worth the suffering it sometimes entailed. Refusing to make commitments means we remain closed in on ourselves. Yet it is only in self-giving that we find ourselves, and only by opening ourselves to others, to children, only by letting ourselves be changed through suffering, do we discover the breadth of our humanity. When such commitment is repudiated, the key figures of human existence likewise vanish: father, mother, and child—essential elements of the experience of being human are lost.[5]

Men learn how to be gentle and tender when they become fathers; so often I have seen this transformation. They learn to compromise—that their way is not always the right way—and how to be responsible. I love watching fathers playing with their kids, teaching a son or daughter how to ride a bicycle, holding their hands when crossing the street, or carrying them on their backs. Boys especially need the example of a father in their lives. They need to learn how to be a man.

Mothers who carry their children during the long months of pregnancy and nourish their children out of their own substance have a special bond. In the night, they hear the cries of their infants unheard by others. They rise uncomplainingly to nurse a baby, encourage their awakening minds, and celebrate their triumphs large and small. No one makes a better confidant than a mom. Like God, they are always there for you. The joy they experience in playing with a young son or daughter is evident on their faces.

Mothers also introduce a child to God, teaching him or her to pray, to trust in God's mysterious presence. In the Gospels, Mary and Joseph present the infant Jesus to the Lord in the temple, making the prescribed offerings (Luke 2:2–40). There is an analogy here with baptism, which, more than a washing away of sin, initiates a child into the Christian community. Baptism cannot be a mere rite of passage. It takes a real commitment on the part of the child's parents, a promise to share their own faith with this child God has given them so that he or she will come to know Jesus and his Father, can recognize his presence in the bread and wine, and learn to serve others in his name. Children also learn much from growing up in loving families. They learn how to look out for younger siblings, to be big brothers or sisters rather than little emperors, like so many boys in China who grow up under the country's "one-child" policy today.

SYNOD ON THE FAMILY

Pope Francis's concern for the health of families was evident in his summoning the International Synod of Bishops to address family life in two sessions, an Extraordinary General Assembly of the Synod of Bishops in October 2014 and a General Assembly of the Synod a year later. As the Extraordinary Synod opened, he encouraged the bishops to speak honestly, listen with humility, and receive with an open heart what others might say. The discussion was free and wide-ranging, with cardinals and bishops publicly taking different positions, sometimes even in the media, for example, on questions of marriage and sexuality, including sexual orientation, civil marriage and cohabitation, and the possibility of admitting those in second marriages without an annulment to communion. The Catholic Church hadn't seen such open and free discussion since the Second Vatican Council.

At the 2015 Ordinary General Assembly of the Synod, some of the most moving testimonies were from those living in interchurch or interfaith families, lay participants able to participate in the language groups but not vote. Given the increasing cultural and religious pluralism today, the example of those who come from different religious traditions was particularly important. They spoke of respecting the religious freedom of their spouses, of coming to appreciate and love their religious traditions, and of learning how to celebrate their common lives and their intercommunity differences. One said that the "differences of religion were never a deterrent for us, for little magic words like compromise, humility, and sorry helped us to lose our ego and live for the other."[6]

The Final Report of the Synod (October 24, 2015), in addressing how to pastorally accompany wounded or broken families (chapter 3), suggests that the Synod's attitude can be characterized by four words: *discernment, accompaniment, integration,* and *reconciliation.* Discernment involves asking, where is this family before God? Accompaniment means learning how to take care of each family, particularly those in difficulty. Integration means that the Church should always seek to include rather than exclude those divorced and civilly married. And reconciliation involves helping to heal wounds and bring those who have been divided together.

Pope Francis has shown special concern for those families divided by divorce. If the traditional nuclear family, with a father and mother together is the ideal, there are other, nontraditional families who also are part of the community of the Church. One of the synod fathers argued that too often the theme of the synod was reduced to that of marriage. He pointed out that today "there are families with only one parent, families without parents, families that include the grandparents, families of grandchildren without parents, families separated by migration—as well as 'religious families' and other forms of living together."[7] Julie Hanlon Rubio, in an article titled "Ordinary, Holy Families," suggested that the Church's emphasis on the "Holy Family" can be off-putting for those whose families are less than ideal. She cites Pope Francis, whose post-synodal apostolic letter "The Joy of Love" (*Amoris laetitia*) points out that the gospel is full of the messy reality of family life, and that indeed, these imperfect or "irregular" families are often models of mercy.[8]

AMORIS LAETITIA

"The Joy of Love" shows a special concern for these irregular situations, stressing both conscience and discernment. Acknowledging that the Church finds it hard "to make room for the consciences of the faithful, who very often respond as best they can to the Gospel amid their limitations, and are capable of carrying out their own discernment in complex situations," the Pope adds, "We have been called to form consciences, not to replace them" (no. 37). The way of the Church is not to condemn but to show mercy, to avoid judgments that fail to take into account the complexity of various circumstances (no. 296), reaching out to the divorced and remarried, to those in civil marriages or simply living together, or those in same-sex relationships, helping them to understand the divine pedagogy of grace, so that they might be able to reach the fullness of God's plan for them (no. 297).

Not all were pleased with the pope's letter. Some felt it was sowing confusion in the Church, with its emphasis on the primacy of conscience and its tendency to treat moral absolutes as "rules" rather than as binding moral obligations. There has been considerable pushback. Others, identifying with Cardinal Christoph Schönborn, who represented the pope in presenting the letter to the press on April 8, 2016, stressed the novelty of the letter, its emphasis on conscience rather than a legalistic approach to moral theology, and its call for a more pastoral approach to those in imperfect situations. Still others were disappointed that the pope did not go further. While he urged respect for those who are homosexual, he did not change Church doctrine or embrace same-sex marriage. But the pope's intention is not to change doctrine—which must be the work of the whole Church—but to change attitudes, so that the Church might better exhibit the mercy that he insists is the "way of Jesus" (no. 296). This is to address real family values, so different from those one hears from those schooled in the Cultural Wars.

The Letter to the Colossians spells out some of these family values:

> As God's chosen ones, holy and beloved, clothe yourselves with compassion, kindness, humility, meekness, and patience. Bear with one another and, if anyone has a complaint against another, forgive each other; just as the Lord has forgiven you, so you also must forgive. Above all, clothe yourselves with love, which binds everything together in perfect harmony. And let the peace of Christ rule in your hearts, to which indeed you were called in the one body. (Col 3:12–15)

23

PRIESTHOOD

> Since, then, we have a great high priest who has passed through
> the heavens, Jesus, the Son of God, let us hold fast to our
> confession. For we do not have a high priest who is unable to
> sympathize with our weaknesses, but we have one who in every
> respect has been tested as we are, yet without sin.
>
> —Hebrews 4:14–15

The Letter to the Hebrews speaks of Jesus as high priest who, in offering prayers and supplications, became the source of salvation for all who obey him (cf. Heb 5:7–10). First Peter also calls all the baptized "a chosen race, a royal priesthood, a holy nation, God's own people, in order that you may proclaim the mighty acts of him who called you out of darkness into his marvelous light" (1 Pet 2:9). But the New Testament never speaks of Christian ministers as priests.

MINISTRY

The word *ministry* comes from the Greek *diakonos/diakonia*, "servant" and "service." It was adopted for those who exercised roles of authority and leadership in the early churches most probably because Jesus chose to describe himself as a servant, as one who came not to be served, but to serve (Mark 10:45; cf. Luke 22:27). The classic illustration is John's picture of Jesus washing the feet of his disciples at the Last Supper (John 13:3–17). The language and iconography of leadership in the Church does not connote power, command, or use conventional terms for authority. Those who exercise leadership roles in the community are called leaders, presiders, pastors, and teachers, later elders and overseers, from which come the English words *presbyters* and *bishops*.

Bishops are overseers, shepherds, or pastors (Latin for *shepherd*). They carry a shepherd's staff, not an officer's baton. A group of presbyters, literally elders, was an inheritance of the synagogue, where they constituted an advisory board of older men. The New Testament frequently refers to presbyters and bishops as one office (Acts 20:17; 1 Pet 5:1–4; 1 Tim 3:8–12; I Clement). As early as Ignatius of Antioch (c. 96), the threefold ministry of a bishop, assisted by presbyters and deacons, was in place at Antioch. By the end of the second century, it was present virtually throughout the Church.

PRIESTHOOD

The development of the language of priesthood is more complex. The Greek *hiereus* and Latin *sacerdos* referred to cultic ministers, "priest" in the popular sense. In the third century, sacerdotal language began to be used of Christian ministers, first of the bishop, shortly after, of presbyters. Even earlier, the *Didache* (c. 100) calls the wandering prophets who celebrated Eucharist "high priests" (13.4). The prayer of consecration attributed to Hippolytus of Rome refers to the bishop as high priest, while Tertullian and Cyprian also speak of the bishop as *sacerdos*. Later, the term was extended to presbyters when referred to together with the bishop.

While the Reformation rejected the language of priesthood for Christian ministers on the basis of the New Testament, the language was most probably adapted because of the bishop's role in presiding at the Eucharist, the memorial of the sacrifice of Christ. Sacerdotal language has kept the nature of the Church as a eucharistic community in full view; where it was dropped, the centrality of the Eucharist often disappeared as well. The English word *priest* comes etymologically from the Greek *presbuteros*, "elder." It carries the meaning of both cultic minister and elder.

According to 1 Peter, echoing Exodus 19:6, the whole community is priestly, consecrated to God, a holy priesthood called to offer spiritual sacrifices (1 Pet 2:5). From the time of the Reformation, Protestant theology has emphasized this universal or baptismal priesthood of all the faithful. Vatican II reclaimed it for Catholics. The Catholic Church had already described bishops as sharing in Christ's threefold office of prophet, priest, and king (language originally from John Calvin); Vatican II applied it to all the faithful: the "faithful are by baptism made one body with Christ and are constituted among the People of God; they are in their own way made sharers in the priestly, prophetical, and kingly functions of Christ; and they carry out for their own part the mission of the whole Christian people in the Church and in the world" (LG 31). The post–Vatican II period saw an explosion of lay ministries in the Church. Yet Pope Francis argues in *Evangelii gaudium* that an excessive clericalism makes many of the laity unable to speak and to act in their particular churches, keeping them away from decision-making (no. 102).

The Constitution on the Church stresses that both the common priesthood of the faithful and the ministerial or hierarchical priesthood are interrelated; each is a participation in the one priesthood of Christ. Ordained priests acting in the person of Christ make present the eucharistic sacrifice, offering it to God in the name of all. The faithful in virtue of their royal priesthood join in offering the Eucharist; "they likewise exercise that priesthood in receiving the sacraments, in prayer and thanksgiving, in the witness of a holy life, and by self-denial and active charity" (LG 10).

PRIESTHOOD AND SACRIFICE

Note that the Council treats the baptismal priesthood in a eucharistic context; in speaking of prayer, thanksgiving, self-denial, and the witness of a holy life, the Constitution echoes 1 Peter's reference to offering spiritual sacrifices. But what does this mean concretely? The Eucharist recalls and proclaims Jesus's life lived in obedience to his Abba, Father, obedient even unto his death on the cross. For this reason, the tradition has spoken of the Eucharist as a sacrifice; Jesus's life is given up for you, poured out as the new and eternal covenant, for you and for many for the forgiveness of sins. This is not to suggest that God demanded a bloody sacrifice as the price of our salvation; Jesus's whole life was a sacrifice of obedience to his Father.

While the New Testament uses many metaphors to express the mystery of salvation, the tradition has given quasi-magisterial status to Anselm's theory of satisfaction, seeing the death of Jesus as the price paid for our salvation, rather than taking into account the whole mystery of his life, his proclamation of the nearness of the kingdom, his concern for the poor and the suffering, his death, and his resurrection. Instead, Anselm reduces the mystery of salvation to some transaction performed through the sacrifice and death of Jesus on the cross, bringing about a change in our relationship to God.

Ronald Rolheiser says that we are washed clean by Jesus's blood. But this does not mean that Jesus paid off some debt owed to God on account of our sins; "God does not keep a scorecard and does not need a bank balance. Rather Jesus' death washes us clean by revealing the heart of a God whose love is faithful enough to not let us die, to open our graves and empty our cemeteries, even when in ignorance or malice we go on killing God and each other."[1]

When we join in offering the Eucharist, we join our own sacrifices to the self-offering of Jesus, memorialized in the words of consecration or institution narrative. The gifts of bread and wine are not just food for the feast; they represent the offering of our lives, to be laid on the altar with the gifts. We bring our own struggles, perhaps care for an aging parent or a difficult child, our efforts to make a marriage work, our struggle with faith or sometimes with the Church, the loneliness that we patiently bear, efforts for integrity at work or in our relationships— these are the "spiritual sacrifices" that we join to the sacrifice of Christ memorialized in the Eucharist. For Pope Benedict XVI, this is the deepest meaning of our "active participation" in the liturgy, not taking on different liturgical roles, but entering into the great Eucharistic Prayer of thanksgiving for God's action of creation and redemption, entering into the institution narrative or consecration that "transubstantiates" the elements of the Earth, joining Christ's offering with our own, with our own obedience to the Father, so that his sacrifice becomes our own. In this way, we "may be transformed into the Logos (logisiert), conformed to the Logos, and so be made the true Body of Christ."[2] The Eucharist invites us to become one with Christ's offering of himself, as he becomes one with us in holy communion. And so the baptismal priesthood offers the sacrifice of holy lives, offered to God as Jesus offered his life for all.

What is the role of the ordained priest? The role of the ordained or ministerial priest is to serve the priesthood of the entire Church; they preach the gospel, shepherd the faithful, and celebrate divine worship (LG 28). In 1997, the priests of Los Angeles held a Priests Assembly with their archbishop, Cardinal Roger Mahony. At the end, the cardinal proposed a letter on priesthood, but the priests asked instead for a letter on ministry, a more inclusive concept embracing both the priests and the faithful. The cardinal agreed; he set up a committee comprised of representatives of the priests of the archdiocese, including two of the auxiliary bishops, and some local theologians to draft an outline of the letter. The resulting pastoral letter on ministry, *As I Have Done for You*, appeared in 2000.

SHARING IN THE ONE PRIESTHOOD

The letter began by contrasting a hypothetical parish, St. Leo's in 1955 and fifty years later. The first St. Leo's had a pastor and two full-time assistant pastors, plus two priests from a local religious community to help on weekends. Only priests could distribute holy communion. The parish had fifteen hundred families. Most of the parish work was sacramental, educational, and devotional. There was a school with a large group of sisters. The liturgy was in Latin, preaching was not biblically based, and though there was some diversity, the priests assumed that everyone spoke English. The parish had few paid employees, a janitor, a housekeeper in the rectory, a parish secretary, and a part-time choir director and organist. There were few meetings for parishioners during the week, except for the Legion of Mary, the Holy Name Society, and the Altar Society that took care of the linens.

By 2005, St. Leo's congregation had grown to five thousand Catholic households, with a large number being Hispanic and Asian. The parish staff now is mostly lay; the parish has a pastor, a lay pastoral associate who is a married laywoman, a permanent deacon, and a large staff of lay ministers, full-time, part-time, and volunteers. The pastor celebrates Mass in both English and Spanish, making some of the older parishioners resentful, while one "supply" priest says Mass in Vietnamese. Morning Mass is celebrated on Mondays, Wednesdays, and Fridays. Full-time staff members include the lay pastoral associate, a liturgy director, youth minister, and director of religious education. St. Leo's School has one sister and a young layman is principal; the teachers are all lay.

With an emphasis on all sharing in the one priesthood of Christ, each evening sees a different ministry or program meeting on the parish grounds; they include the Parish Council, a food pantry, an outreach to the elderly, marriage preparation classes conducted by two married couples, and another class for adult faith formation. The young adult group gathers on Friday evenings; there is also a charismatic prayer group, a Cursillo group, and several self-help groups based on the Twelve-Step Program. Another group takes communion to the sick and the shut-ins. An ecumenical group is trying to find ways to reach out to neighboring congregations.

The snapshots of St. Leo's Parish in 1955 and 2005 give a good idea of how parish life up to the present time has changed. And so has the understanding of the priest's role. Prior to the Second Vatican Council, the role of the priest was seen primarily from a cultic perspective; ordination gave him "sacred power" (*sacra potestas*) to "confect" the Eucharist. The priest was a man apart with an assumed superior holiness based on his cultic role; his life was centered on the Eucharist. Though this view dominated seminary formation down to the Second Vatican Council, the Council itself moved beyond this cultic model of priesthood, to stress instead ministry. In the document on the ministry and life of priests, *Presbyterorum ordinis*, the word *ministry* (*diakonia*) appears more than forty-five times and there is a strong emphasis on the ministry of the word.

Lumen gentium emphasized that both the ordained and baptismal priesthood share in the one priesthood of Christ, but it failed to develop how the two priesthoods are related. Cardinal Mahony's letter addresses that question: "The purpose of priestly ordination is to call forth and serve the priesthood of the whole Church, the entire Body."[3] The ordained both engage the priesthood of the faithful and represent the priesthood of Christ to the priestly people. Their lives are ordered to prayer, witness, and service on behalf of the whole Church. As coworkers with the bishop, the priest is a sign of ecclesial communion, drawing together all the baptized into communion and mutual service. Because priests have been authorized to act in the name of the Church, they act *in persona Christi capitis*, in the person of Christ the head of the Church. The ordained priest serves God's priestly people.

PART V
LIVING THE GOSPEL

24

THE GIFT OF
CONTEMPLATION

M ost Catholic undergraduates today have no idea who
Thomas Merton (1915–68) was, let alone why he was
an important figure in twentieth-century American Catholicism. But
Merton inspired several generations of Catholics, teaching them that
contemplative prayer was not just for the professionally religious, for
cloistered monks and nuns, but a grace or gift that God offers to many.

THE YOUNG MERTON

Long a person without a real home, the child of two artists,
Merton grew up on both sides of the Atlantic. His mother was an
American who died of cancer when he was six, his father a painter from
New Zealand with no religious background; he too died when Merton
was sixteen. A brilliant but somewhat unsettled student, young Tom
attended primary school at a lycée in France, high school at Oakham
in England, and began his university studies at Cambridge, only to
be called home in disgrace in 1934 by an uncle, his guardian, apparently after getting a young woman pregnant. He enrolled at Columbia

University to continue his studies where his talent as a writer began to emerge.

While at Columbia, he began to experience an attraction to Catholicism, almost against his will. He had been fascinated by the art he saw in the churches of Italy, and Etienne Gilson's *The Spirit of Medieval Philosophy* influenced him profoundly, introducing him to a philosophical concept of God that made sense, though he almost threw the book from the window of the train carrying him home to Douglaston when he saw it had an imprimatur, signifying that it was a Catholic book. Initially interested in Eastern religions, at the suggestion of a Hindu monk, Bramachari, he began to read some Christian classics, including Augustine's *Confessions* and the *Imitation of Christ*. He was baptized on November 16, 1938, at Corpus Christi Church in New York. Shortly after his conversion, he tried to enter the Franciscans, but was turned down, no doubt because of his past.

While teaching at St. Bonaventure College (now University) in western New York, Dan Walsh, a philosophy professor he had met while working at Catherine de Hueck Doherty's Friendship House in Harlem, suggested that he make a Holy Week retreat at Gethsemani, a Trappist abbey in Kentucky. Arriving at the monastery long after dark, he was led to his room by the brother guestmaster. Immediately, Merton was moved by the place. As he writes in his famous autobiography, "And I felt the deep, deep silence of the night, and of peace, and of holiness enfold me like love, like safety."[1]

THE MONK

That December at the age of twenty-six, three days after the attack on Pearl Harbor, he entered the community. Gethsemani at that time was one of the strictest houses in the order. The monks slept in their habits in a common dormitory, rose at 2:00 a.m. for the first office of the day, and returned six more times before Compline brought the day to a close. Their life was austere in the extreme. But Merton was happy; for the first time he had found a home.

Brother Louis, as he was now known, thought he had left the writer behind him. In *The Seven Storey Mountain*, which appeared in 1948, he complained about "this shadow, this double, this writer who had followed me into the cloister. ... And the worst of it, he has my superiors on his side."[2] His early works were pious lives of Cistercian saints, works celebrating the monastic life, and some poetry. He rejoiced over his escape from "the world," and some of his works seemed to suggest that the monastic life was the only path to holiness. But Merton continued to grow and to change.

In a famous passage, he describes an experience in 1958, a graced moment that marked an important transition in his life: "In Louisville, at the corner of Fourth and Walnut, in the center of the shopping district, I was suddenly overwhelmed with the realization that I loved all those people, that they were mine and I theirs, that we could not be alien to one another even though we were total strangers. It was like waking from a dream of separateness, of spurious self-isolation in a special world, the world of renunciation and supposed holiness."[3] It was as though his eyes had opened to take in the troubled world that now intruded into his monastic seclusion.

Merton had left his isolation behind, even as he continued his monastic life. This sense of seeing the world with new eyes would continue to characterize his approach to contemplation. In subsequent years, he would emerge as a contemplative critic, publishing articles against war, in favor of civil rights, ecology, and nonviolence, many of them in Dorothy Day's *The Catholic Worker*. He became a quasi-unofficial chaplain to the peace movement during the Vietnam War.

MERTON AND CONTEMPLATION

Along with his social involvement, Merton continued to write on contemplation. This had always been his primary interest. He tells us in his famous autobiography that when he was about four, to his mother's confusion, he had "a deep and serious urge to adore the gas-light in the kitchen, with no little ritualistic veneration."[4] As a young monk, he studied the rich contemplative tradition of the church. One of his first works, *Seeds of Contemplation*, first published in 1949, was basically a series of notes and personal reflections on the interior life. While still very traditional, stressing the differences between nature and grace, the natural and supernatural dimensions of spirituality, Merton was already showing signs of placing greater emphasis on experience. Not satisfied, he continued to rework his manuscript.

In 1962, he published *New Seeds of Contemplation*, one of his finest books. Like Ignatius of Loyola, whose final exercise in the *Spiritual Exercises*, the *Contemplatio ad Amorem*, shows the retreatant how God can be found in all things, Merton writes of how we are surrounded by signs of God's love that can move us deeply into prayer, drawing us into contemplation. It may be a meditation, gazing at a crucifix, or sitting quietly in the presence of the Blessed Sacrament. Or it may be the beauty of nature. In a lyrical passage, he writes,

> For it is God's love that warms me in the sun and God's love that sends the cold rain. It is God's love that feeds me in the bread I eat and God that feeds me also by hunger and fasting. It is the love of God that sends the winter days when I am cold and sick, and the hot summer when I labor and my clothes are full of sweat: but it is God Who breathes on me with light winds off the river and in the breezes out of the wood. His love sends the water-boy along the edge of the wheat field with a bucket from the spring, while the laborers are resting and the mules stand under the tree.[5]

All these "seeds of contemplation" awaken us to God's mysterious presence. But contemplative prayer is not busy; it is a quiet prayer of attentiveness and waiting. It is not a trance or ecstasy, not the hearing of unutterable words, not the emotional fire and sweetness that come with religious exaltation. It is neither enthusiasm nor a sense of being "seized," nor is it an escape from conflict or doubt. When God draws one into this contemplation, our response should be simply to rest quietly in God's presence: "we ought to remain at peace in a prayer that is utterly simplified, stripped of acts and reflections and clean of images, waiting in emptiness and vigilant expectancy for the will of God to be done in us," waiting without anxiety, and without a hunger for any special experience.[6] We rest in a kind of darkness, our busy minds quiet, our imagination stilled.

Yet experience is the way into contemplation. According to Merton, it is not easily taught or explained. It can only be suggested, pointed to, or symbolized. He argues that contemplation arises from the transcendent self that subsists before the eyes of God, so different from the superficial "I." It is not the illusory person, who exists outside the reach of God's will and God's love. Our superficial self has no permanence; it is neither eternal nor spiritual, but doomed to disappear. The secret of my identity, he says, is hidden in the love and mercy of God. This is the "true self" united to God in Christ.

In contemplation, we come to discover that we are already in union with God, to find ourselves caught up in the Divine Mystery. "A door opens in the center of our being and we seem to fall through it into immense depths which, although they are infinite, are all accessible to us."[7] We come to see that God is not a *what* or a *thing*, but rather a *who*, a Thou "before whom our inmost 'I' springs into awareness."[8]

Once in a letter to one of his many correspondents, Merton describes his own prayer in intimate terms:

> Now you ask about my method of meditation. Strictly speaking I have a very simple way of prayer. It is centered entirely on attention to the presence of God and to His will and His love. That is to say that it is centered on *faith* by which alone we can know the presence of God....Yet it does not mean imagining anything or conceiving a precise image of God, for to my mind that would be a kind of idolatry....My prayer is

then a kind of praise rising up out of the center of Nothing and Silence. If I am still present "myself" this I recognize as an obstacle. ... Such is my ordinary way of prayer, or meditation. It is not "thinking about" anything, but a direct seeking of the Face of the Invisible. ... I do not ordinarily write about such things and ask you therefore to be discreet about it.[9]

Throughout his monastic life, Merton felt a call to greater solitude. For a while he thought of joining the Carthusians, though his abbot helped him discern that his place was at Gethsemani. Appointed Master of Novices in 1955, he had the novices build a cottage of cinder blocks about a mile from the monastery, a place for retreatants and ecumenical discussions, but Merton saw it as a hermitage where he could spend time alone. In 1965, he finally received permission to live there full time, and resigning from his duties with the novices, he moved in.

FINAL JOURNEY

Early in 1968, Merton received an invitation from an international Benedictine group to take part in a conference for Asian Benedictine and Cistercian monastics in Bangkok and to give the principal address. The new abbot, Dom Flavian Burns, gave him permission to go. In a letter circulated to his friends in September, he expressed the hope that his trip to Asia would "also enable me to get in contact with Buddhist monasticism and see something of it firsthand."[10] He was going, not as a research scholar or writer, but "as a pilgrim who is anxious to obtain not just information, not just 'facts' about other monastic traditions, but to drink from ancient sources of monastic vision and experience."[11] To this end he made arrangements to meet with a number of Buddhist monks known as spiritual masters.

After several stops in the United States, including a visit to Our Lady of the Redwoods, a Trappistine community on the Pacific coast, he finally departed San Francisco for Bangkok on October 15. In Dharamsala, accompanied by Harold Talbott, an American student of Buddhism, he spent five days visiting the Dalai Lama. From there he visited several Buddhist monks in Tibet and Ceylon (now known as Sri Lanka). At Polonnaruwa, before the famous statue of the "Sleeping Buddha," he had a spiritual experience, describing it as a moment of inner clarity that moved him greatly.

From there he went to Singapore, and then Bangkok, where on December 10, he gave his paper. Following a siesta that afternoon and coming out of the shower, he was electrocuted after touching an electric fan that had a defective wire. He died twenty-seven years to the day he had entered the order. He was fifty-three years old.

At the end of his famous autobiography, Merton wrote, "Whether you teach or live in the cloister or nurse the sick, whether you are in religion or out of it, married or single, no matter who you are or what you are, you are called to the summit of perfection: you are called to a deep interior life perhaps even to mystical prayer, and to pass the fruits of your contemplation on to others. And if you cannot do so by word, then by example."[12]

25

THE TRUE SELF

Every morning, we encounter our own face staring back at us from the bathroom mirror. But who is it that we see there? Do we recognize the image? Is it someone we know well? Is it the public *persona* that we present to others? Are we able to see our true self, even in its morning disarray?

We all find ourselves with different *personae*. We move in different circles, sometimes changing aspects of our personality to accommodate them. Sometimes we wonder who we really are. At times we are not even sure where our own deepest identity lies. We see only the failings, our own sinfulness, our inability to respond to grace. We are aware of missed opportunities, of long struggles and old wounds, and of things we'd like to change. There are aspects of ourselves we do not like. We do not always see the good. We want to discover our true self, which lies hidden.

Little children are different; they are wonderful, so spontaneous. Their joy or sorrow is immediately evident, faces exuberant, reflecting the joy of being alive, or covered with tears. Their honesty is sometimes startling; their feelings are not hidden, but transparent. Their eyes are bright, curious, and full of trust. If they consider you a friend, they greet you with love and open arms. They say the most amazing things, to our amusement or sometimes regret. If their identity is inchoate, their personality is already emerging. Regrettably, when they grow older they become self-conscious. Their spontaneity disappears, and they become inarticulate about what they are really feeling. Teenage girls giggle; boys become awkward or withdrawn. They are not always aware of why they react the way they do. The passage to adulthood is often long and tortuous.

DISCOVERING ONE'S IDENTITY

Mature adults are those who have developed a system of values that shapes their behavior. They are able to integrate their affectivity with those values and their personal commitments. They are not dominated by their feelings, but neither do they repress or deny them. They have a sense of identity—personal, vocational, and sexual. They are capable of love and lasting friendships. Honesty and personal integrity are important to them; once lost, regaining either is difficult. Still, the true self can remain mysterious.

One of the values of the Catholic practice of sacramental confession is that it provides an opportunity to acknowledge failings and the need for growth. It is not difficult to admit that one is a sinner. But it is much more difficult to say, I was dishonest, took advantage of someone, abused another, or destroyed his or her reputation. We gain insight into ourselves. Sometimes who we really are emerges in moments of challenge or crisis.

Recently, I was teaching in Shanghai. On the way home, after paying the taxi driver, I discovered as soon as I entered the Pudong Airport lobby that I had left my wallet in the cab. In it were more than five hundred American dollars—the reimbursement for my plane fare—and several hundred dollars in Chinese RMBs. Plus my credit cards, driver's license, and so on. I ran back to the curb, but the cab was gone. I tried to explain my predicament at several Air China counters, but no one spoke adequate English. Resigned to having to cancel credit cards, get a new driver's license, and to having lost the cash, I had about twenty minutes before my flight, when a young woman from the airline beckoned me to come with her. We went through the lobby, past some airport shops, back through security, and there at the door, a big smile on his face and my wallet in his hands was the cab driver.

Here was a man of integrity. He had found the wallet, come back, found a place to park his taxi in spite of the traffic, and brought it to security for the airline. I tried to give him a few hundred RMB notes, but he refused, shaking my hand and waving good-bye.

Thomas Merton, first as master of scholastics, later as master of novices, was concerned that the young monks he sought to form develop an authentic sense of identity. Like so many of their peers, many of these young men came into the monastery from an often dehumanizing culture with little sense of who they were. They thought that life in the monastery might help them resolve their identity issues, but for Merton the monastic life presumed an authentic identity; the monastery was not the place to find it.

He argued that to have an identity was to witness to the truth in one's own life. Each monk had to discover that for himself. But this was a personal, existential issue, not something found through conformity to monastic rules or traditions. Each monk had to become a responsible, mature member of the community, not passive or just seeking approval from superiors. They had to be capable of mature human relationships. Just to be the "good religious" who never breaks the rules or strayed from the norm was insufficient. Conversely, one did not mature simply by rebelling against authority. The first alternative absolves one from thinking and responsible behavior; the other is adolescent.

Key for Merton was for each monk to attain a sense of authenticity and personal integrity. For the contemplative life, a lack of identity is a disaster. The search for God cannot be divorced from discovering one's own inner truth. Conformity to external observances is not enough. An important sign of discovering and affirming one's identity, with the necessary acceptance of oneself as willed by God, is the understanding and acceptance of the solitary character of the monastic life.[1]

THE TRUE SELF

Merton takes up the same theme, though on a deeper level, in is writings on contemplation. In his *New Seeds of Contemplation*, he sought to distinguish the superficial "I," the ego or exterior, empirical self from the true self. The ego forms a kind of mask; it is self-constructed—he calls it an illusion. The true self cannot be reduced to the soul; it includes both body and soul. The Genesis myth of the fall teaches us that we have been exiled from God (Gen 3), and thus from our true self. The Christian life is about the return to the Father through the Son in the Spirit. For the contemplative, the superficial "I" sometimes drops away and the true self, united with God, the inmost "I," comes into awareness.[2]

In another work, never quite finished and published posthumously, Merton argues that the conviction that we are created in the image of God means that the inner self is a "mirror" in which God is reflected and revealed: "Through the dark, transparent mystery of our own inner being we can, as it were see God 'through a glass.' All this is of course pure metaphor. It is a way of saying that our being somehow communicates directly with the Being of God, Who is 'in us.'" Much as Merton appreciated the religions of the east, especially Zen, he found a significant difference between Christianity and Zen precisely here: "In Zen there seems to be no effort to get beyond the inner self. In Christianity the inner self is simply a stepping stone to an awareness of God."[3]

Discovering one's true identity is not just an issue for young monks. Each of us must move beyond the pseudoselves, shaped by advertising and a consumerist culture, telling us that our well-being is shaped by what we have, showing us all the things we need to be happy, creating unreal needs. Such a culture makes things more valuable than relationships. We have to have the latest iPhone, the newest flat screen television set, the most sophisticated computer, the sexiest car. Online merchants monitor our tastes and preferences with "cookies," sending us e-mails about products we might be interested in, and they are often right. Amazon.com is aware of what books I would like to read before I am.

I've been fascinated with the multiplication of "storage units," long sheds with retractable, corrugated metal doors, painted orange or blue or green, springing up in vacant lots in our cities or along our freeways. Their popularity suggests a culture in which no one ever throws anything away. We cling to things acquired until we have to rent places to store them.

To discover our true selves, we need spiritual freedom. St. Ignatius of Loyola calls this "indifference" toward material possessions and personal concerns. In the "First Principle and Foundation" at the beginning of his *Spiritual Exercises,* he says that "the human person is created to praise, reverence, and serve God Our Lord, and by doing so, to save his or her soul.... It follows from this that one must use other created things, in so far as they help toward one's end, and free oneself from them, in so far as they are obstacles to one's end. To do this, we need to make ourselves indifferent to all created things." This does not mean a lack of care for the things of this world, for the beauties of nature or the joys of friendship or the works of human creativity, but only that nothing should come between us and God.

Spiritual freedom demands more than not being attached to things. It also demands an inner freedom, a willingness to face our fears, deal with unresolved issues, and be honest first of all with ourselves, which is always the most difficult. It implies being willing to act on what a truthful assessment reveals. It is not an easy process. It might mean change, which is rarely easy. But it also means that we are on the way to letting our true self emerge.

One of my longtime friends was someone with whom I shared a good deal. Over the years, when we shook hands I noticed that his hands were always damp. I wondered about this. Was it constitutional, or was he nervous about something? I didn't know and thought it was just natural. But it was years after we first became acquainted that he told me that he was gay. I was surprised, and we talked about it a bit. This was not just the first time he admitted his sexual orientation to me;

it was also the first time he had really admitted it to himself. But the next time we shook hands, sometime later, I noticed that his hands were no longer damp. They were warm and dry.

"Coming out" for my friend was a big step in his own life. He had some help from another gay member of the community. There he found insight and support; still it took some courage. It didn't change our relationship; we were still close. He was still the same, sober brother, faithful to his vows and to his commitment. He didn't publicly identify as a gay man, still less as a gay priest. But to those closest to him, he was honest. His public *persona* and the truth he knew about himself were congruent. Spiritually, he was able to bring himself before God as the person he was. With his new sense of self, his true self was beginning to appear. There was an authenticity or integrity about him, which means being and owning the person God created him to be.

The Christian tradition tells us that our gracious God is present in the very depths of our souls, far below the superficial "I," the masks we often wear. There we find the God who holds us in a loving embrace.

26

THAT THEY MAY BE ONE

One of our campus ministers told us a story of a young woman he was preparing for a retreat; let's call her Consuelo. Born in Mexico, the girl's father died when she was three years old and her mother moved to the United States to support her, faithfully sending checks to the child's grandmother who was raising her. A devout Catholic, the grandmother shared her own strong faith with the girl and she embraced it willingly. After ten years, the mother arranged to have Consuelo come to the States to join her.

But right away there were tensions in her new home. Her mother had remarried and had another daughter and a son with her new husband. He was a Pentecostal, and she had joined his church. Now they wanted Consuelo to convert and join their church also. The girl, committed to her Catholic faith, refused. With considerable pressure from her new family, the tension in the home became too great; she found little peace there and spent most of her teenage years living with some of her new friends from school. How sad that confessional differences can so divide a family, separating those who should be brothers and sisters in the Lord.

LOSS OF COMMUNION

How did these divisions in the Body of Christ come about? For most of the first millennium, the various churches—local churches under their bishops or patriarchs—lived in communion, though there were differences in theology, spirituality, liturgy, and law between the churches of the Latin West and those of the East. As early as 96, Ignatius of Antioch referred to the church of Rome as the church "which presides in love," while in 180, Irenaeus of Lyons held it up as the church with which all should agree in doctrinal matters because of her "more powerful origin" (*potentiorem principalitatem*), having not just one but two apostolic founders, Peter and Paul. Even before the fourth century, when Roman bishops began appealing to a greater authority or primacy based on Peter, other churches would appeal to Rome as a court of appeal or focus of unity.

The first breaks in communion occurred after the councils of Ephesus (431) and Chalcedon (451). The Assyrian Church or Church of the East, once stretching from the Mediterranean to China, the Coptic, Ethopian, Eritrean, Syriac, Malankara, and Armenian churches, known today as the Oriental Orthodox, lost communion with the Latin West and the other Eastern churches in a dispute over developing christological language. Most would henceforth be known as Monophysite, "one nature," in their theology. An even greater break came in 1054 when communion between the Greek-speaking Eastern (Orthodox) churches and the Latin West was lost when Cardinal Humbert, the leader of the papal legation to Constantinople and the Patriarch of Constantinople, Michael Cerularius, excommunicated each other in a dispute over jurisdiction, though theological, jurisdictional, and canonical differences had long been developing.

The communion of the Western Church was shattered with the Reformation in the sixteenth century. Starting with the Lutherans in

Germany, the Reformation spread to the Reformed or Calvinist tradition under John Calvin and Ulrich Zwingli in Switzerland and later France, the Netherlands, Hungry, Transylvania, and Scotland, and the English church's break with Rome in 1534, resulting in a separate Church of England, later the Anglican communion. On the Reformation's left wing were the Anabaptist communities such as the Swiss Brethren, the Hutterites, the Mennonites, and later the Amish; this "Radical Reformation" attempted to reconstitute the Church on the model of the New Testament. Many of them were peace churches, and still are today. But once the charism of unity was lost, the churches continued to divide.

The Catholic Church, too, has experienced losses. Some Catholics in Austria, Germany, Holland, and Switzerland broke with Rome over the issue of papal infallibility in 1870 to form the Old Catholic Church. In the United States, Polish immigrants, frustrated with the lack of Polish bishops and without Polish language instruction in their parishes established the Polish National Catholic Church in 1897. According to the Center for the Study of Global Christianity at Gordon-Conwell Theological Seminary, in 1900 there were sixteen hundred denominations. Today the number is roughly forty-three thousand.

ECUMENICAL MOVEMENT

So what has happened to the Body of Christ? It is fractured, broken, divided. The modern ecumenical movement traces its beginnings from the World Missionary Conference at Edinburgh, Scotland, in 1910. The meeting brought together representatives of Protestant churches, mostly from North America and northern Europe; the Orthodox and Catholic churches had not been invited, and most likely would not have come if they had been. An outgrowth of the Protestant missionary movement, the focus of the conference was not on Christian unity but on practical cooperation in mission. Could the churches cooperate in preparing biblical translations, distributing Bibles and

Christian literature, even work together in the Church's Evangelical mission? But as the twelve hundred delegates began addressing these questions, others arose: Why are we divided? Is this what the Lord wanted for his Church? This was the beginning of the movement for Christian unity, the ecumenical movement, and many of those who took part at Edinburgh constituted the first generation of ecumenists.

The next step forward, tracing its roots to the Edinburgh conference, was the First World Conference on Faith and Order at Lausanne, Switzerland, in 1927. The conference sought to address divisions between the churches based on *faith*—doctrine and theology—as well as *order*—polity or church structure (papal-episcopal, episcopal, presbyteral, congregational, or free church). At this stage, the Catholic Church was still not interested in this new movement toward unity, fearing that it represented an ecclesiological relativism that looked on ecclesiological differences as unimportant. In 1928, Pope Pius XI responded with an encyclical *Mortalium animos*, forbidding Catholic participation: "So, Venerable Brethren, it is clear why this Apostolic See has never allowed its subjects to take part in the assemblies of non-Catholics: for the union of Christians can only be promoted by promoting the return to the one true Church of Christ of those who are separated from it, for in the past they have unhappily left it" (no. 10). In other words, the only kind of ecumenism acceptable for Catholics was an ecumenism of return.

The next important step was the formation of the World Council of Churches (WCC) at Amsterdam in 1948. This time, some of the Orthodox churches joined in as founding members, while some Catholics were unofficially present as observers. The Faith and Order Conference became an important commission within the WCC and today includes Catholic members. The WCC is not a church, but a free association or fellowship of churches that remain autonomous, but work together in the cause of Christian unity. Today, there are some 348 member churches in the WCC. Two of the Faith and Order Commission's most important achievements are the convergence statements: *Baptism, Eucharist and Ministry* (1982), often referred to as the "Lima Text" or simply as BEM, and *The Church: Towards a Common Vision*

(2013). Not so much statements of agreements among the churches, they represent a consensus of theologians from the different traditions. But they stand as a challenge for the renewal of all the churches.

The Catholic Church's official entrance into the ecumenical movement came with the Second Vatican Council; indeed, in calling the Church into council, Pope John XXIII stated as one of his two goals a "renewed invitation to the faithful of the separated communities that they also may follow us amiably in this search for unity and grace, to which so many souls aspire in all parts of the earth."[1] The Council's Decree on Ecumenism (*Unitatis reintegration*) expressed the Catholic Church's commitment to the ecumenical movement and principles for its conduct. It recognizes the ecclesial status of the Orthodox churches that it sees as having preserved the apostolic succession and true sacraments. Most other non-Catholic churches it regards as "ecclesial communities" of Christians, united with Christ, consecrated by baptism, living in his Spirit, nourished by the word of God, and celebrating other sacraments. They possess constitutive elements of the Church that incorporate their members into the Body of Christ; link them to other Christians through the life of grace and the theological virtues of faith, hope, and charity; and are capable of leading them to salvation (see LG 15; UR 3, 22). Their marriages are considered sacramental and their celebrations of the Lord's Supper mediate grace. The 1993 ecumenical *Directory* recognizes these churches and ecclesial communities as retaining "a certain communion" with the Catholic Church.[2]

The goal of the ecumenical movement is not a megachurch but the restoration of ecclesial communion between and among the divided churches. Since the Council ended, the Catholic Church has established formal bilateral and multilateral dialogues with most of the world's Christian churches and traditions, including Evangelicals and Pentecostals. While progress has been slow, it has been considerable, as through study and conversation, the churches have found new ways of looking at historically divisive issues and considerable agreement on what unites them.

So where are we today? Fr. John Hotchkin (d. 2000), one of the premiere Catholic ecumenists in the United States, once described the ecumenical movement as being in its "Third Stage."[3] The first stage was one of reaching out, getting to know each other, and making friends. Ecumenism always begins in friendship. When we get to know someone from another Christian church or tradition, then they no longer remain a stranger, the religious "other," but become a brother or sister in Christ.

The second stage is the stage of dialogue, of exploring where we have differences and often discovering how much we actually have in common. The Catholic Church has been in dialogue since the Council ended in 1965. Perhaps the three most significant ecumenical statements are Vatican II's Decree on Ecumenism (1964) and the two WCC texts mentioned earlier, *Baptism, Eucharist and Ministry* (1982) and *The Church: Towards a Common Vision* (2013). Also most important is the 1999 Lutheran-Roman Catholic Joint Declaration on the Doctrine of Justification, the issue that first divided the churches in the sixteenth century.

The third stage involves taking positive steps toward reconciliation and full communion. Some churches have already taken those steps, for example, Anglicans and Lutherans (ELCA) in the United States, the Anglican and Lutheran churches of Great Britain and Ireland, and the Lutheran national churches of the Nordic countries as well as the Baltic churches of Estonia and Lithuania. Full communion means basic agreement in doctrine and the ability to exchange ministers and share together in the Eucharist.

My students consistently refer to friends who are Lutherans or Evangelicals as belonging to "another religion," rather than another Christian church. Baptism establishes a bond between all Christians, in the words of Vatican II, an imperfect communion. Ecumenism seeks to make the communion full, but we are all members of Christ's Body, the Church, even if we belong to different ecclesial traditions. A good friend of mine, an Evangelical Christian, was sent by his Church with his wife on a mission to France, to convert the French. While he liked the people he met, he found them adrift religiously; many would say something like, "I am French. I am Catholic. I believe in reincarnation. I am an atheist. I am a scientist. I go to a healer when I am sick. I am a rationalist."[4]

He began a Bible study with several of them, and when they were ready to accept Jesus, he said it was time to start a church. But they said, we're French, and Catholic; come to our church. Somewhat hesitantly he did, and while standing with the congregation in prayer, he suddenly began to sense the presence of God's Spirit. He was completely rattled, because as a good Evangelical, he did not expect to experience the Holy Spirit at a Catholic Mass. The Spirit was not supposed to be there. The same thing happened the next time he went to Mass. Finally, he went to see the priest, and they had a long conversation. After some further conversations, prayer, and discernment, he decided his mission would be better served by helping his new French friends become better Catholic Christians rooted in Christ, than to start another church. After all, their culture was Catholic, not Evangelical. So for the next twenty years, he and his wife worked as Evangelical members of their Catholic parish.

The tragedy in Consuelo's story with which we began was that neither seemed able to recognize and respect the other's faith. Think of the terrible divisions today in the Muslim community between Sunni and Shiites, with often murderous animosities that go back centuries. Divisions in the Body of Christ are a scandal; they are obstacles to the Church's Evangelical mission. It is easy to dismiss another Christian community, in order to build up one's own. We have all been guilty of this at times. This is not to deny that Catholics have some special claims to an apostolic distinctiveness. But Christ's Church is not exhausted by the Catholic Church.

What we need is an ecumenical spirituality that recognizes our common origin in baptism and our common discipleship. We need to find Christ in our brother or sister. For Pope Francis, to work for ecumenism is to be peacemakers, among those whom Jesus called blessed (Matt 5:9); to be a peacemaker is to contribute to the unity of the human family (EG 244).

Thomas Merton's famous autobiography reflects the enthusiasm and often the intolerance of the new convert when he speaks of other Christian traditions. There is a triumphal character about the way he talks about Catholicism. But the mature Merton was much more inclusive in his approach to Christian diversity. In his *Conjectures of a Guilty Bystander*, he wrote,

> If I can unite *in myself* the thought and devotion of Eastern and Western Christendom, the Greek and Latin Fathers, the Russians with the Spanish mystics, I can prepare in myself the reunion of divided Christians. From that secret and unspoken unity in myself can eventually come a visible and manifest unity of all Christians. If we want to bring together what is divided, we cannot do so by imposing one division upon the other or absorbing one division into the other. But if we do this, the union is not Christian. It is political, and doomed to further conflict. We must contain all divided worlds in ourselves and transcend them in Christ.[5]

27

The Church and the Jews

In June 1960, Jules Isaac, a French Jewish historian who had lost his wife and daughter in the Holocaust, had a meeting with Pope John XXIII. Isaac had long investigated the historical roots of anti-Semitism, most notably in his 1948 book, *Jésus et Israël*. John XXIII had just announced that he was summoning the Church into council. In their private meeting, Isaac asked the pope to have the Council, which was then in its planning stages, address the question of the Church and the Jews, summarizing what he called "the teachings of contempt" for Jews and Judaism.

A TRAGIC HISTORY

The history of Christian-Jewish relations is too often tragic, even violent. It includes the charge of "deicide," persecutions, pogroms, and slanders such as the myth of Jewish ritual murder of Christian children, and the anti-Jewish writings of some of the Church fathers. St. John Chrysostom's theology could be described as a form of anti-Jewish supercessionism, the view that, because the Jews of Jesus's time had failed to recognize him as the Messiah, the Church had replaced Israel as God's chosen people. Peter the Venerable was quite anti-Semitic.

St. John Capistrano was called "the scourge of the Jews." There were periods of great tragedy. In 1096, during the First Crusade, it is estimated that up to ten thousand Jews were killed by mob violence in Mainz, Cologne, Treves, Neuss, Regensburg, Prague, and other cities along the Rhine, the Danube, and in northern France, even though many bishops sought to protect them.

In preaching the Second Crusade, Bernard of Clairvaux insisted that the Jews not be harmed, but still there were massacres throughout Germany and France. In his book *The Anguish of the Jews*, Edward Flannery argues that the popes were the Jews' best defenders, though he does not include Innocent III, whose restrictive policies, including requiring distinctive dress for Jews and Saracens, were made law by the Fourth Lateran Council in 1215.[1] Rome was the only large European city from which the Jews were never expelled, and they generally enjoyed good relations with their neighbors in Italy, though there were exceptions.

Pope John understood Isaac's concerns and responded graciously. He was not unacquainted with Jewish suffering. During the war he had served as apostolic delegate in Turkey and Greece and had gone out of his way to assist Jews fleeing Nazi persecution, providing them with bogus baptismal certificates, visas, and false identity papers, to help them reach Palestine. Shortly after his election to the Chair of Peter, he ordered that the Good Friday prayer for the "perfidious Jews" be removed from the Catholic ritual. To ensure that the Council addressed the Church's relation to the Jews, he called on Jesuit Cardinal Augustin Bea, prefect of the recently created Secretariat for Promoting Christ Unity, to make it happen.

NOSTRA AETATE

The result was *Nostra aetate*, the Declaration on the Relation of the Church with Non-Christian Religions. Its history is complicated. At first, the Secretariat proposed the topic of Jewish-Catholic relations be taken up as part of the Decree on Ecumenism. Later, the bishops voted for a separate document. Finally, they decided to include the relations of the Church to the other world religions as well.

The declaration was groundbreaking. Besides acknowledging that the Church recognized that the other world religions "often reflect a ray of that Truth which enlightens all [people]" and encouraging dialogue (NA 2), the Declaration completely reframed the way the Church looked at the Jews. Gone was the old theology of contempt, and left behind as well was the supercessionist teaching. Using the language of St. Paul, the declaration speaks of the Church drawing "sustenance from the root of that well-cultivated olive tree onto which have been grafted the wild shoots, the Gentiles" (cf. Rom 11:17–24). Nor can a supercessionist theology be presented as biblical. "Although the Church is the new people of God, the Jews should not be presented as rejected or accursed by God, as if this followed from the Holy Scriptures." Speaking of God's promise to Israel, the declaration states that "God holds the Jews most dear for the sake of their Fathers; He does not repent of the gifts He makes or of the calls He issues—such is the witness of the Apostle" (NA 4).

The declaration also dealt implicitly with the ancient charge of deicide, the idea that the Jews, in putting Jesus to death, were guilty of killing God, a charge too often used in the past to taunt Jewish children, in spite of the fact that the Council of Trent said in the sixteenth century that *all* human beings were to be regarded as Christ's crucifiers. Specifically, *Nostra aetate* teaches that though "the Jewish authorities" pressed for the death of Jesus, "still, what happened in His passion cannot be charged against all the Jews, without distinction, then alive, nor against the Jews of today." It firmly rejected anti-Semitism of any kind: "The Church, mindful of the patrimony she shares with the Jews and moved not by political reasons but by the Gospel's spiritual love, decries hatred, persecutions, displays of anti-Semitism, directed against Jews at any time and by anyone" (no. 4).

ANTECEDENTS

A fascinating book by John Connelly, *From Enemy to Brother: The Revolution in Catholic Teaching on the Jews 1933–1965*, traces how deeply rooted anti-Judaism and, indeed, racism were present in some parts of the Catholic Church in the first half of the twentieth century.[2] It is painful to read how Catholic intellectuals and scholars, including several Jesuits, regularly taught that the Jews carried a defect in their genes for the sin of rejecting Jesus and therefore lived under a curse, often traced to Matthew 27:25, the cry of the crowd: "His blood be on us and on our children!" Not even baptism could remove the effect of this sin, and so Jewish converts had to "work hard" to undo its effects. This theological anti-Judaism sat well with the Nazi ideology and its emphasis on race, blood, and people (*Volk*). Tragically, some Catholics in Germany sought to be bridge-builders between the two ideologies.

Connolly shows how this tradition of Catholic anti-Judaism was gradually reversed. Among the first to argue that God's promise to the Jews was irrevocable was the French novelist and convert León Bloy. But Connolly's real focus is on how the language ultimately used by the Council was developed by a group of anti-Nazi Catholics in central Europe shortly after Hitler came to power, most of whom were born Jewish. Turning to Paul's Letter to the Romans, in which Paul wrestles with the question of why his own people were unable to recognize Jesus as Messiah and Lord, they reclaimed his language. Before the war, some had used Paul to argue that the Jews could become good Christians through baptism, but without it, they could not escape the curse. Especially influential was Johannes Oesterreicher, a Jewish convert from Moravia, ordained in 1927. He founded the Pauluswerk in Vienna for Jewish converts to Catholicism. After the *Anschluss*, he fled to France, and then to New York. Named as a theological advisor to the Council, he was one of the authors of *Nostra aetate*.

In the postwar period, a new generation joined Oesterreicher to reject the very idea of a curse. Karl Thieme, originally from a family of Protestant theologians, converted to Catholicism in 1934. Around

1950, he began to argue, citing Bloy, that the Jews remained beloved by God precisely as Jews. In October 1964, Gregory Baum and Bruno Hussar, both converts from Judaism, joined Oesterreicher in drafting a statement that became the Council's decree on the Jews. Especially contentious was the question of whether or not the Church should evangelize the Jews. Thieme and later Oesterreicher came to see that, given God's irrevocable covenant with Israel, that a mission to the Jews was no longer appropriate. The Council, moved by the statement of Rabbi Abraham Heschel that he was "ready to go to Auschwitz any time, if faced with the alternative of conversion or death," dropped any mention of the conversion of the Jews. *Nostra aetate* provided the theological foundation for a new relationship between the Church and the Jews; it was enormously significant in beginning the process of reconciliation.

POPE JOHN PAUL II

It was Pope St. John Paul II who more than anyone else made that reconciliation a reality. Having grown up in Krakow, as a youth he had Jewish friends who perished in the Shoah. One of the most moving is the story of his friend Jerzy Kluger. Jerzy and John Paul, then Karol Wojtyla, grew up together in Wadowice. They hiked and played soccer together and helped each other with their homework. The war separated the two friends and they lost touch. After the Germans invaded Poland, Kluger fled with his father, ending up in Russia, and later serving with Polish troops in Africa and in the Italian campaign where he met his wife, Irene White, a driver for the British Army. His mother and sister died at Auschwitz. With no family left in Poland, Kugler studied engineering in England after the war, finally settling in Rome. During the Second Vatican Council, he read about a talk by a Polish bishop by the name of Wojtyla. He called and the bishop returned his call immediately, and they renewed their friendship. After Wojtyla was elected pope, his first audience was with Kugler and his family, and Kugler was one of his last visitors before the pope died in 2005.

John Paul was the first pope to visit a death camp, and the first to visit a synagogue. At the Rome Synagogue on April 13, 1986, he said, "The Jewish religion is not 'extrinsic' to us but in a certain way is 'intrinsic' to our religion. With Judaism, therefore, we have a relationship which we do not have with any other religion. You are our dearly beloved brothers, and in a certain way, it can be said that you are our elder brothers." He condemned anti-Semitism, affirming the validity of Jewish faith and of God's covenant with the Jews. In 1994, he officially recognized the state of Israel and, in March 1998, promulgated "We Remember: A Reflection on the 'Shoah,'" eleven years in preparation. The document acknowledged anti-Judaism on the part of many Christians, as well as sins and failures of Christians, including Church leaders against the Jews. Perhaps most moving was John Paul's prayer in 2000 before the Western Wall, following a visit to Yad Vashem, Israel's memorial to the victims of the Holocaust. Now an old man and ill with Parkinson's disease, he placed his own prayer between the fissures in the great wall, once the foundation of the temple.

To mark the beginning of the third millennium, the International Theological Commission under John Paul's leadership published "Memory and Reconciliation: The Church and the Faults of the Past." The document called for a purification of memory and a collective examination of conscience for faults committed by the sons and daughters of the Church, among them the use of force in the pursuit of the truth, the inquisition, and the crusades; forced evangelization in the Americas; and sins against the Jews over the centuries. He asked if the anti-Jewish prejudice embedded in some Christian minds and hearts had not made the Nazi persecution easier, acknowledging that Christians had not done all they might have to help their Jewish neighbors.

It is difficult to deny that centuries of what Jules Isaac called "the teaching of contempt" contributed to the horrors of the Holocaust. The Shoah is only one of numerous genocides in the twentieth century.

Even today religious fundamentalism and the inability to recognize a brother or sister in the religious "other" continues to lead to outbreaks of terrorism. Why are our hearts so often closed to the other, to those who are different in race, religion, ethnicity, sexual orientation, gender, or social condition? Please, God, give us inclusive hearts.

28

Our Fragile Home

One of the many benefits of the first space flights to the moon in the late 1960s was those beautiful pictures of planet Earth taken by the astronauts, that blue globe swathed in clouds floating in the vast blackness of space. The very perspective of those pictures changed for many their sense for our home; it seemed small, fragile even. Indeed it is, as we have learned. The Earth is under threat from abuse and neglect, and we are responsible.

LAUDATO SI'

No one has addressed that more powerfully than Pope Francis in his encyclical on the environment, *Laudato si'* (2015). The encyclical is not primarily about climate change as is so often alleged, though climate change is one of his concerns. Rather, it is an encyclical on our "common home," or as St. Francis of Assisi would say, our Sister, Mother Earth, who now cries out to us because of the harm we have inflicted on her by our irresponsible use and abuse of the goods with which God has endowed her.

The encyclical is very long: 246 paragraphs, 163 pages, divided into six chapters, but its concreteness and lack of abstract jargon, unlike most encyclicals, makes it an easy read. Two themes are woven throughout. First, we belong to one human family, dependent on each other, and we are related to all other living beings. Second, the ecological crisis calls for a fundamental change in our lifestyles.

The Pope calls attention to how we have plundered and abused the Earth; filling it with filth and waste, poisoning her atmosphere, cutting down the forests that purify her air, and polluting her life-giving streams and the oceans rich with living creatures. People get sick from insecticides, fungicides, herbicides, and agro toxins. Each year we generate millions of tons of waste, much of it nonbiodegradable, toxic, even radioactive. These problems are closely linked to a throwaway culture. Most of the paper we produce is thrown away, not recycled, and our industrial system has not developed the capacity to absorb and reuse the waste and by-products it produces. Think, for example, of nuclear waste or the pollution problems today in poor countries where raw sewage runs out of houses and down the streets. There are many premature deaths. Children are especially vulnerable.

In 2012, an estimated 8.4 million people died from air, water, and land pollution, according to the Global Alliance on Health and Pollution; "pollution alone kills three times more people than HIV, malaria, and tuberculosis combined."[1] The World Health Organization reports 7 million premature deaths annually from air pollution alone. Many people do not have access to safe drinking water, which the pope notes is being turned into a commodity. More than sixteen hundred children die every day from diseases caused by drinking unsafe water. Access to safe drinking water is a basic human right, not something subject to the laws of commerce. We forget that not just Gringos get sick in Mexico from the water; millions of children suffer from the same problem. Francis asks, Have we no concern for coming generations?

On top of this, there is the warming of the climatic system due to the concentration of greenhouse gases that come from human activity. Recent studies show that the great concentration of greenhouse gases (carbon dioxide, methane, nitrogen oxides, and others) released as a result of human activity, are concentrated in the atmosphere; they do not allow the warmth of the sun's rays reflected by the Earth to be dispersed in space. The intensive use of fossil fuels aggravates the problem. Africa especially is vulnerable. We need to progressively replace highly polluting fossil fuels, especially coal, but also oil. This is not new teaching! Pope Paul VI, Pope John Paul II, and Pope Benedict all called for policies to mitigate greenhouse gas emissions and assist those most affected by the harmful effects of climate change.

The abuse of the environment affects all of us, but especially the poor, particularly the quarter of the world's population that lives on the coasts or nearby, and it contributes to the massive migration taking place today. Those nations that have benefited from industrialization at the cost of an enormous increase in greenhouse gases have a greater responsibility toward providing a solution. An "ecological debt" exists between the global north and south, due to commercial imbalances.

The encyclical addresses every person living on the planet, thus other churches and Christian communities, other religions, all people of good will. Francis is concerned that we are exploiting the rich resources of our planet, with thousands of plant and animal species disappearing every year. He says that "because of us, thousands of species will no longer give glory to God by their very existence" (no. 33). Acknowledging that the Church does not have all the answers, he calls repeatedly for dialogue. He wants to draw on the best scientific research available to us today. But saving the planet involves all of us, not just the scientific community. Pope Francis says, "Our goal is not to amass information or to satisfy curiosity, but rather to become painfully aware, to dare to turn what is happening to the world into our own personal suffering and thus to discover what each of us can do about it" (no. 19).

A TRINITARIAN VISION

Chapter 2 of *Laudato si'* is especially beautiful. Here, this Jesuit pope is at his most Franciscan. The Bible teaches the immense dignity of each person, created in the image and likeness of God and declared good by the Creator. From a biblical perspective, Pope Francis argues that human life is grounded in three fundamental and closely intertwined relationships: with God, with our neighbor, and with the Earth itself. These three vital relationships have been broken, both outwardly and within us. According to Genesis 3, this rupture is the result of sin, the sin of our presuming to take the place of God and refusing to acknowledge our creaturely limitations.

We cannot address the problems of our planet without reshaping our relationships with God, our neighbors, and the Earth. From a Christian perspective, the pope's vision here is profoundly trinitarian; God is not a distant, solitary watchmaker but a loving Father who brings all things into being through the Word and fills creation with his life-giving Spirit. Thus, the Earth is not our own; we do not have absolute dominion over the Earth, which belongs to God alone. We are caretakers, not owners.

In speaking of evolution, Francis notes the "sheer novelty involved in the emergence of a personal being within a material universe," which suggests the action of God and a particular call to life on the part of a "Thou" who also addresses human beings in this highly personal way (no. 81). He writes, "It is clearly inconsistent to combat trafficking in endangered species while remaining completely indifferent to human trafficking, unconcerned about the poor, or undertaking to destroy another human being deemed unwanted," speaking of life in the womb (no. 91). He also argues that the Bible does not support a tyrannical anthropocentrism at the expense of other creatures. Ecologists, long skeptical of anthropocentrism at the expense of the environment, have been delighted with this emphasis.

Chapter 3 calls for not just a heightened environmental consciousness, but also for a substantial change in the way we live, which means to change our lifestyles, our habits of consumption and methods of production, all of which contribute to climate change, a global problem with environmental, social, and economic consequences. Scientific and technological progress cannot be equated with the progress of humanity. This was also a constant theme of Pope Benedict XVI, as, for example, in his encyclical on hope, *Spe salvi*. But the pope is not antiscience. Technoscience, when properly directed, can improve the quality of human life; he says, "Who can deny the beauty of an aircraft or a skyscraper?" (*Laudato si'* 103).

The basic point of chapter 4 is that as human beings, we belong to one single human family, dependent on each other and on the Earth that is our common home. As the pope repeats numerous times, all things are connected and dependent on one another.

> Time and space are not independent of one another, and not even atoms or subatomic particles can be considered in isolation. Just as the different aspects of the planet— physical, chemical and biological—are interrelated, so too living species are part of a network which we will never fully explore and understand. A good part of our genetic code is shared by many living beings. (no. 138)

We are becoming more aware of the importance of how different creatures relate to one another in making up the larger units that we call "ecosystems." We depend on these systems for our own existence; "we need only recall how ecosystems interact in dispersing carbon dioxide, purifying water, controlling illnesses and epidemics, forming soil, breaking down waste, and in many other ways which we overlook or simply do not know about" (no. 140). *Sustainable use* means considering each ecosystem's regenerative ability. We need to be in solidarity with each other, and care for the Earth, not exploit it.

Nature can no longer be regarded as something separate from ourselves or as a mere setting in which we live. We are part of nature, included in it and thus in constant interaction with it. The environmental crisis is one, affecting nature and society, the social and the environmental. Nor can we continue to ignore the poor. He writes that "a true ecological approach *always* becomes a social approach; it must integrate questions of justice in debates on the environment, so as to hear *both the cry of the earth and the cry of the poor*" (no. 49). Human ecology is inseparable from the principle of the common good, the central and unifying principle of Catholic social ethics. It includes being concerned for the lack of housing and public transportation, and for extreme poverty. When I see films on global poverty and realize those disadvantaged peoples are also seeing films about our affluence, I wonder what will happen when they begin to demand their fair share, and I fear for the future.

Chapter 5 outlines some lines of approach and action in dealing with the environmental crisis. Francis acknowledges that the Church does not presume to answer scientific questions, but is concerned about an honest debate, bringing politics and the economy into dialogue. The environment will not be safeguarded by a free market, profit-driven economy. He is not calling for an end to capitalism, but for a spirituality more sensitive to our hurting planet. We may have to accept decreased growth in some parts of the world so that poorer regions may begin to flourish. He calls for a new, integral, and interdisciplinary approach to politics, one which will no longer tolerate organized crime, human trafficking, the drug trade, and violence. Religion has its own role to play, opening new horizons, especially since the majority of people on the planet profess to be believers.

AN ECOLOGICAL SPIRITUALITY

The final chapter calls for education in ecology and for a spirituality to support a new lifestyle. The pope challenges what he calls the "myths" of modernity—individualism, the myth of ongoing progress, consumerism, and unregulated free markets. In his 2013 encyclical *Evangelii gaudium*, he pronounced a firm no to an economy of exclusion and inequality. He argues,

> Some people continue to defend trickle-down theories which assume that economic growth, encouraged by a free market, will inevitably succeed in bringing about greater

justice and inclusiveness in the world. This opinion, which has never been confirmed by the facts, expresses a crude and naïve trust in the goodness of those wielding economic power and in the sacralized workings of the prevailing economic system. Meanwhile, the excluded are still waiting. (no. 54)

In *Laudato si'*, he contrasts such a "utilitarian mindset," characterized by consumerism, competition, and an unregulated market, with an environmental education that seeks to recover levels of ecological equilibrium, with one's self, in solidarity with others, and with God.

An environmental education should strive to embrace the transcendent, thus giving environmental ethics their deepest meaning; at the same time, it should help develop an "ecological citizenship," encouraging us to reduce water consumption, separate refuse, cook only what can reasonably be consumed, use public transportation or carpooling, plant trees, turn off unnecessary lights, and so on. We can each do something.

Some who ridicule expressions of environmental concern need an "ecological conversion." Care for nature includes a capacity for living together and in communion with others, in a kind of "universal fraternity." In a beautiful passage, he says that the "universe unfolds in God, who fills it completely. Hence, there is a mystical meaning to be found in a leaf, in a mountain trail, in a dewdrop, in a poor person's face.... to discover God in all things" (no. 233).

Pope Francis's encyclical is both poetic and practical: he reminds all to say grace before meals, reminding us that our food comes from the Earth. Running throughout it are the strategic principles of gradualism and incrementalism. We cannot solve everything at once; still we need to get started. He stresses repeatedly the importance of dialogue. More dangerous to a doctrinal relativism is a practical relativism that gives absolute priority to our immediate convenience. Interestingly, Francis avoids the language of a culture of life and a culture of death, so often used by Pope John Paul II. He does not want to discount the values that may be present in contemporary culture.

The pope's Catholic, communitarian sensibility is obvious throughout the encyclical. He writes that the fruits of the Earth are meant to benefit everyone. The climate, our atmosphere, and the Earth's natural resources are goods held in common, "belonging to all and meant for all." He argues that the Christian tradition has never recognized the right to private property as absolute or inviolable, and has stressed the social purpose of all forms of private property. The fathers of the Church said that the poor man has the right to take from those who have more than they need for his own needs (GS 69). Similarly, he rejects the idea that national sovereignty is an absolute right; we need instead global regulatory norms. I wonder how many would welcome his teaching today.

While advancing the Catholic tradition, the encyclical remains rooted in it. Thus it rejects population control as a means to address the environmental crisis and stresses the unique difference, transcending biology, between humans and animals, even if experimentation on animals is permissible when it contributes to saving human lives (no. 130). It argues that gendered differences should be respected and differentiates God from creation, which in the Eucharist is "projected towards divinization…towards unification with the Creator himself," suggesting that our beautiful Earth is to be included in God's plan of salvation (*Laudato si'* 236).

The Jesuit paleontologist Teilhard de Chardin had a similar vision. In *The Phenomenon of Man*, he envisions a cosmic evolution that moves from the realm of matter (*geosphere*) to life (*biosphere*), and ultimately thought (*noosphere*). While a strictly materialist narrative leaves no room for God or God's Spirit, reducing life and mind to the merely physical, Teilhard's vision looks further. He sees that some kind of transformation has been going on since the beginning in the complexification of the material. There are more atoms in the human eye than there are stars in the known universe.

As evolution continues, it moves toward a larger, more dramatic future, through stages of life, mind, and eventually a global self-consciousness as the simultaneity of modern communications increasingly reduces the physical distance between peoples and nations. Teilhard would have been fascinated by the internet, which functions today as a global nervous system, sharing information and linking people together. Thus, his vision sees the material world as becoming increasingly spiritual, moving toward that union with God in the cosmic Christ he calls Point Omega. Similarly, Ilia Delio says that we meet Christ not just in faith but also at the heart of the evolutionary process; we meet him "in the divine, continual act of creation, redemption, and sanctification of the total universe."[2] For both, Christ is the beginning and the end of all unity in the cosmos.

Thus that beautiful globe we marvel at in those pictures from space is more than spaceship Earth, our planetary home. It is a womb in which is growing a communion of diverse peoples united in Christ and with the Creator whose light and life has called them into being from before time began. Francis's encyclical *Laudato si'* is a beautiful meditation on the damage we are doing to the Earth and a call to the conversion necessary to save our common home. A Christian spirituality should encourage a prophetic and contemplative lifestyle; it should not be obsessed with consumption. This is Pope Francis at his most Franciscan!

Notes

PART I. GOD

1. The Holy

1. Rudolf Otto, *The Idea of the Holy* (London: Oxford University Press, 1950).

2. Robert Neelly Bellah and Richard Madsen, *Habits of the Heart* (Berkeley: University of California Press, 1996), 221.

3. Wade Clark Roof, *Spiritual Marketplace: Baby Boomers and the Remaking of Religion* (Princeton: Princeton University Press, 1999); see also *A Generation of Seekers: The Spiritual Journey of the Baby Boomer Generation* (San Francisco: HarperCollins, 1993).

4. Walter Kasper, *Mercy: The Essence of the Gospel and the Key to Christian Life* (New York: Paulist Press, 2014), 84.

5. Ibid., 52.

6. Tertullian, *The Chaplet*, 3, http://www.earlychristianwritings.com/text/tertullian04.html.

7. Andrew Greeley, *The Catholic Imagination* (Berkeley: University of California Press, 2000), 1.

8. Thomas Merton, *New Seeds of Contemplation* (New York: New Directions, 2007), 82.

9. Dorothy Day, *The Long Loneliness: The Autobiography of the Legendary Catholic Social Activist* (San Francisco: HarperSanFrancisco, 1952), 84.

2. Beauty

1. Frederick Buechner, *The Sacred Journey* (San Francisco: Harper & Row, 1982), 52.

2. Pope Francis, "Papal Message to Russian Orthodox Choir That Sang in Rome," Zenit, November 5, 2013, https://zenit.org/articles/papal-message-to-russian-orthodox-choir-that-sang-in-rome/.

3. John Paul II, "Letter to Artists," (1999); he appeals to the Septuagint Greek translation of the first Genesis Creation story, where Hebrew "good" is translated by the Greek *kalón*, beautiful.

4. Cecilia González-Andrieu, *Bridge to Wonder: Art as a Gospel of Beauty* (Waco, TX: Baylor University Press, 2012), 22–23.

5. Richard Viladesau, *Theological Aesthetics: God in Imagination, Beauty, and Art* (New York: Oxford University Press, 1999), 150.

6. Ibid., 20.

7. Andrew Greeley, *The Catholic Imagination* (Berkeley: University of California Press, 2000), 76.

3. Silence

1. William George, "Learning Alone," *America* 199, no. 7 (2008): 16.

2. Carlo Maria Martini, "Teaching the Faith in a Postmodern World," *America* 196 (2008): 20.

3. Thomas Merton, *Entering the Silence: Becoming a Monk and Writer*, vol. 2 of *The Journals of Thomas Merton, 1941–1952*, ed. Jonathan Montaldo (San Francisco: HarperCollins Publishers, 1996), 185–86.

4. Brian O. McDermott, "With Him, In Him: The Graces of the Spiritual Exercises," *Studies in the Spirituality of Jesuits* 18, no. 4 (1986): 24.

5. Thomas Merton, "The Identity Crisis," in *Contemplation in a World of Action* (Notre Dame, IN: University of Notre Dame Press, 1998), 79.

6. Joseph Ratzinger, *Feast of Faith: Approaches to a Theology of the Liturgy* (San Francisco: Ignatius Press, 1986), 73.

7. Catherine of Siena, *Gratiarum actio ad Trinitatem*, cap. 167.

8. Gerhard Lohfink, *Does God Need the Church?* (Collegeville, MN: Liturgical Press, 1999), 259–60.

4. Evil

1. John Paul II, *Crossing the Threshold of Hope*, ed. Vittorio Messori (New York: Random House, 1994), 61. Emphasis in the original.

2. John F. Haught, *God and Darwin: A Theology of Evolution* (Boulder, CO: Westview Press, 2008), 54.

3. Etty Hillesum, *An Interrupted Life: The Diaries, 1941–1943; and Letters from Westerbork* (New York: Henry Holt, 1996), 151; first published in 1981.

4. Walter Kasper, *Mercy: The Essence of the Gospel and the Key to Christian Life* (New York: Paulist Press, 2014), 2.

5. Hope

1. Walter Hooper, *C. S. Lewis: Companion and Guide* (San Francisco: HarperSanFrancisco, 1996), 25.

2. Dag Hammarskjöld, *Markings* (New York: Vintage Spiritual Classics, 2006), 56.

6. A Love That Endures

1. See Jon Birger, *Date-onomics: How Dating Became a Lopsided Numbers Game* (New York: Workman Publishing, 2015), 23–43.

2. Ibid., 38.

3. Joan Baez, vocal performance of "Love Is Just a Four Letter Word," by Bob Dylan, recorded September 1968, on *Any Day Now*, CBS Studios Nashville.

4. Robert Ellsberg, "Dorothy in Love," *America* (November 15, 2019), http://americamagazine.org/issue/755/ideas/dorothy-love.

5. Michael Downey, *Altogether Gift: A Trinitarian Spirituality* (Maryknoll, NY: Orbis Books, 2000), 54.

6. Augustine, *Tractate* 26.5.

7. Augustine, *Confessions*, I.1. Author's emphasis.

8. See Martin Heidegger, *An Introduction to Metaphysics* (New Haven, CT: Yale University Press, 1959), 18–21.

9. Dorothy Day, *Dorothy Day: Selected Writings,* ed. Robert Ellsberg (Maryknoll, NY: Orbis Books, 2005), 181.

PART II. JESUS

7. Incarnation

1. Cited by Ronald Rolheiser, "In Exile: Christ the King," http://liturgy.slu.edu/ChristKingB2015/reflections_rolheiser.html.

2. Kate Dugan and Jennifer Owens, eds. *From the Pews in the Back: Young Women and Catholicism* (Collegeville, MN: Liturgical Press, 2009), 96–97.

3. Dennis Hamm, "Rummaging for God: Praying Backwards through Your Day," *America* (May 14, 1994), http://www.ignatian spirituality.com/ignatian-prayer/the-examen/rummaging-for-god -praying-backward-through-your-day.

8. The Mother of Jesus

1. See Tim Perry, *Mary for Evangelicals: Toward an Understanding of the Mother of Our Lord* (Downers Grove, IL: InterVarsity Academic,

2006); Scot McKnight, *The Real Mary: Why Evangelical Christians Can Embrace the Mother of Jesus* (Brewster, MA: Paraclete Press, 2007).

2. Andrew Greeley, *The Mary Myth: On the Femininity of God* (New York: Seabury Press, 1977).

3. Raymond E. Brown, *Biblical Reflections on Crisis Facing the Church* (New York: Paulist Press, 1975), 106–7; see also Elizabeth A. Johnson, *Truly Our Sister: A Theology of Mary in the Communion of Saints* (New York: Bloomsbury Academic, 2003).

4. Mary Dixon Thayer wrote more than one poem for Our Lady. This prayer-poem was popularized in the 1950s by Archbishop Fulton Sheen.

9. The Beatitudes

1. Pope Benedict XVI, *Jesus of Nazareth: From the Baptism in the Jordan to the Transfiguration* (New York: Doubleday, 2007), 74.

2. See Walter M. Abbott, *The Documents of Vatican II* (New York: Guild Press, 1966), 716.

3. Walter Kasper, *Mercy: The Essence of the Gospel and the Key to Christian Life* (New York: Paulist Press, 2014), 56.

4. Thomas Merton, *New Seeds of Contemplation* (New York: New Directions, 1972), 18.

5. Pope Benedict XVI, *Jesus of Nazareth: From the Baptism in the Jordan to the Transfiguration* (New York: Doubleday, 2007), 92.

6. Cindy Wooden, "Christians Who Reject All Refugees Are 'Hypocrites,' Pope Says," *Catholic News Service*, October 13, 2016.

7. Carolyn Whitney-Brown, *Jean Vanier: Essential Writings* (New York: Orbis Books, 2008), 105–11.

8. Jean Vanier, "L'Arche: Its History and Vision," in *The Church and the Disabled Person*, ed. Griff Hogan (Springfield, IL: Templegate, 1983), 52.

10. Resurrection

1. From the sermon "Meditating on Christ's Passion" by Pope St. Leo the Great.

2. Thomas Merton, *Contemplation in a World of Action* (Notre Dame, IN: University of Notre Dame Press, 1998), 143.

11. Paschal Mystery

1. Robert P. Imbelli, *Rekindling the Christic Imagination: Theological Meditations for the New Evangelization* (Collegeville, MN: Liturgical Press, 2014), 9.

12. The Imitation of Christ

1. Giles Constable, *Three Studies in Medieval Religious and Social Thought* (New York: Cambridge University Press, 1995), 157.

2. Terrence W. Tilley, *The Disciples' Jesus: Christology as Reconciling Practice* (Maryknoll, NY: Orbis Books, 2008), 187.

3. Susan Bergman, ed., *Martyrs: Contemporary Writers on Modern Lives of Faith* (Maryknoll, NY: Orbis Books, 1998), 15.

4. Weil's first English biographer, Richard Rees, offers several possible explanations for her death, citing her compassion for the suffering of her countrymen in occupied France and her love for and close imitation of Christ. Richard Rees, *Simone Weil: A Sketch for a Portrait* (London: Oxford University Press, 1966), 191.

5. Cited by Kevin Clarke, *Oscar Romero: Love Must Win Out* (Collegeville, MN: Liturgical Press, 2014), 101.

6. "Bonhoeffer on This-worldliness," *Episcopal Café* (April 9, 2013), http://www.episcopalcafe.com/bonhoeffer_on_this_worldliness/.

PART III. THE SPIRIT

13. The Spirit and Grace

1. Brian E. Daley, "The Unexpected God: How Christian Faith Discovers the Holy Spirit" (lecture, Duquesne University, Pittsburgh, PA, September 23, 2011), 23; http://www.duq.edu/Documents/liberalarts/_pdf/337535c%20Holy%20Spirit%20Colloquium%20Lecture%20Booklet%2010.12WEB.pdf.

2. Ibid., 24.

3. See Joel S. Panzer, *The Popes and Slavery* (New York: Alba House, 1996); see also John T. McGreevy, *American Jesuits and the World: How an Embattled Religious Order Made Modern Catholicism Global* (Princeton, NJ: Princeton University Press, 2016), 58, 119.

4. Elizabeth A. Johnson, *Ask the Beasts: Darwin and the God of Love* (London: Bloomsbury, 2014), 179.

5. For example, Walter Kasper used this term in his "The Current Ecumenical Transition," *Origins* 36, no. 26 (2006): 411.

6. Irenaeus, *Against the Heresies*, 5.1.3.

14. Spirituality

1. Robert Wuthnow, *All in Sync: How Music and Art Are Revitalizing American Religion* (Berkeley: University of California Press, 2003), 32.

2. Ibid., 24–25.

3. Ibid., 36.

4. Sandra M. Schneiders, "Religion vs. Spirituality: A Contemporary Conundrum," *Spiritus* 3, no. 2 (2003): 173.

5. Vincent J. Miller, *Consuming Religion: Christian Faith and Practice in a Consumer Culture* (New York: Continuum, 2004), 225–28.

6. Ibid., 106.

7. Ibid., 202.

8. Andrew Greeley, *The Catholic Imagination* (Los Angeles: University of California Press, 2000), 175.

9. Carlo Maria Martini, "Teach the Faith in a Postmodern World," *America* 198, no. 16 (2008): 18.

10. Philip Jenkins, The Next Christendom: The Coming of Global Christianity (New York: Oxford University Press, 2002), 7–8.

11. Renato Poblete, "The Catholic Church and Latin America's Pentecostals," *Origins* 27, no. 43 (1998): 7–8.

12. Jorge Mario Bergoglio, "Religiosidad Popular Como Inculturación de la Fe," *Testigos de Aparecida* 2 (2009): 281–325; English translation, "Traditional Piety as Inculturation of the Faith," in *Family and Life: Pastoral Reflections*, trans. James Crowley (New York: Paulist Press, 2015), 75.

15. The Power of Compassion

1. Greg Boyle, *Tattoos on the Heart: The Power of Boundless Compassion* (New York: Free Press, 2010).

2. "The Slow Work of God" is the title of a prayer by the French Jesuit Pierre Teilhard de Chardin.

16. Reconciliation

1. See http://www.nytimes.com/interactive/2014/04/06/magazine/06-pieter-hugo-rwanda-portraits.html.

17. Salvation

1. Andrew Greeley, *The Catholic Imagination* (Berkeley, CA: Berkeley University of California Press, 2000), 159–70.

PART IV. CHURCH

20. Eucharist

1. Ronald Rolheiser, "Eucharist as God's Touch" (July 14, 1993), http://ronrolheiser.com/eucharist-as-gods-touch/#.V4QPpaInInE.

21. Body of Christ

1. Henri de Lubac, *Corpus Mysticum* (Notre Dame: University of Notre Dame Press, 2006), 79–80, 256–59.

2. Pope Francis, "Homily for the Solemnity of Mary, Mother of God," January 1, 2015.

3. Terrence W. Tilley, *The Disciples' Jesus: Christology as Reconciling Practice* (Maryknoll, NY: Orbis Books, 2008), 236.

4. Dorothy Day, *The Long Loneliness* (San Francisco: HarperSanFrancisco, 1952), 285.

22. Holy Families

1. Statistics for the Center for Applied Research in the Apostolate (CARA); http://cara.georgetown.edu/frequently-requested-church-statistics/.

2. Thomas Reese, "2001 and Beyond: Preparing the Church for the Next Millennium," *America* 176, no. 21 (1977): 11.

3. *Letter to Diognetus*, chap. 5.

4. *Didache* 2.

5. Address of Benedict XVI on the Occasion of his Christmas Greetings to the Roman Curia, December 21, 2012.

6. Synod of Bishops, The Final Report of the Synod of Bishops to the Holy Father, Pope Francis, Vatican City, October 24, 2015, http://

www.vatican.va/roman_curia/synod/documents/rc_synod_doc
_20151026_relazione-finale-xiv-assemblea_en.html.

7. Cited by Antonio Spadaro, "The Vocation and Mission of the Family: The 14th Ordinary Synod of Bishops," *La Civiltà Cattolica* 4 (November 28, 2015): 372–91.

8. Julie Hanlon Rubio, "Ordinary, Holy Families: Looking to the Bible for New Model of Mercy," *America* 214, no. 20 (June 20–27, 2016): 16–19.

23. Priesthood

1. Ronald Rolheiser, "Bringing New Life," *America* 213, no. 9 (October 5, 2015): 16.

2. Joseph Ratzinger, *The Spirit of the Liturgy* (San Francisco: Ignatius Press, 2000), 173.

3. Roger Mahony, *A Pastoral Letter on Ministry: As I Have Done for You* (Chicago: Liturgy Training Publications, 2000), 23.

PART V. LIVING THE GOSPEL

24. The Gift of Contemplation

1. Thomas Merton, *The Seven Storey Mountain: An Autobiography of Faith* (New York: Harcourt, 1998), 352; first published 1948.

2. Ibid., 448–49.

3. Thomas Merton, *Conjectures of a Guilty Bystander* (New York: Doubleday, 1989), 156; first published 1968.

4. Merton, *Seven Storey Mountain*, 6.

5. Thomas Merton, *New Seeds of Contemplation* (New York: New Directions, 1962), 17.

6. Ibid., 240.

7. Ibid., 225–27.

8. Ibid., 13.

9. Thomas Merton, "To Abdul Aziz," in *The Hidden Ground of Love*, ed. William H. Shannon (New York: Farrar, Straus, Giroux, 1985), 63–64.

10. *The Asian Journal of Thomas Merton*, ed. Naomi Burton, Patrick Hart, and James Laughlin (New York: New Directions, 1968), 295.

11. Ibid., 312–13.

12. Merton, *Seven Storey Mountain*, 458.

25. The True Self

1. See Thomas Merton, "The Identity Crisis," in *Contemplation in a World of Action* (Notre Dame, IN: University of Notre Dame Press, 1998), 58–83; first published 1962.

2. Thomas Merton, *New Seeds of Contemplation* (New York: New Directions, 1972), 7–13, 279–87.

3. Thomas Merton, "The Inner Experience," in *Thomas Merton: Spiritual Master*, ed. Lawrence S. Cunningham (New York: Paulist Press, 1992), 302.

26. That They May Be One

1. John XXIII, "Announcement of an Ecumenical Council," January 25, 1959.

2. *Directory for the Application of Principles and Norms on Ecumenism*, no. 18.

3. John Hotchkin, "The Ecumenical Movement's Third Stage," *Origins* 25, no. 21 (November 9, 1995): 353–61.

4. See David E. Bjork, *Unfamiliar Paths: The Challenge of Recognizing the Work of Christ in Strange Clothing* (Pasadena, CA: William Carey Library, 1997), 2.

5. Thomas Merton, *Conjectures of a Guilty Bystander* (New York: Doubleday, 1966), 21, italics in the original.

27. The Church and the Jews

1. Edward H. Flannery, *The Anguish of the Jews: Twenty-Three Centuries of Antisemitism* (New York: Paulist Press, 1985), 102.

2. John Connelly, *From Enemy to Brother: The Revolution in Catholic Teaching on the Jews 1933–1965* (Cambridge, MA: Harvard University Press, 2012).

28. Our Fragile Home

1. Global Alliance on Health and Pollution, "Pollution: The Largest Cause of Death in the Developing World" (April 2016), http://www.gahp.net/new/pollutionthelargestcauseofdeath/.

2. Ilia Delio, *Christ in Evolution* (Maryknoll, NY: Orbis, 2008), 132.